RITUAL AND DEVOTION IN BUDDHISM

Also by Sangharakshita

A Survey of Buddhism
Flame in Darkness
Collected Poems 1941–1994
The Three Jewels
Crossing the Stream
The Essence of Zen
The Thousand-Petalled Lotus
Human Enlightenment
The Religion of Art
The Ten Pillars of Buddhism
The Eternal Legacy
Travel Letters
Alternative Traditions
Conquering New Worlds
Ambedkar and Buddhism
The History of My Going for Refuge
The Taste of Freedom
New Currents in Western Buddhism
A Guide to the Buddhist Path
Learning to Walk
Vision and Transformation
The Buddha's Victory
Facing Mount Kanchenjunga
The FWBO and 'Protestant Buddhism'
The Drama of Cosmic Enlightenment
Wisdom Beyond Words
The Priceless Jewel
Who is the Buddha?
In the Realm of the Lotus
Peace is a Fire
The Meaning of Orthodoxy in Buddhism
Mind Reactive and Creative
Going For Refuge
The Caves of Bhaja
My Relation to the Order
Hercules and the Birds and Other Poems
Buddhism and the West
Forty-Three Years Ago
The Meaning of Conversion in Buddhism
Was the Buddha a Bhikkhu?
The Inconceivable Emancipation
Transforming Self and World

•

SANGHARAKSHITA

•

RITUAL AND DEVOTION IN BUDDHISM

•

AN INTRODUCTION

•

WINDHORSE PUBLICATIONS

Published by Windhorse Publications
Unit 1-316 The Custard Factory
Gibb Street
Birmingham
B9 4AA

Printed by Biddles Ltd, Guildford, Surrey.

Design   Lisa Dedman
Cover design   Dhammarati
Text illustrations   Varaprabha

The cover shows a gilded wooden figure of one of the Buddha's disciples,
from Thailand, photographed by Bruce Rae

British Library Cataloguing in Publication Data
A catalogue record for this book is available from the British Library

ISBN 0 904766 87 X

•

Contents

•

EDITOR'S PREFACE

ANY WESTERN BUDDHIST TODAY has been – or perhaps is still going – through a process of conversion to Buddhism. Even if, like the sixteen-year-old youth who was to become Sangharakshita, you one day realize quite unequivocally that you are a Buddhist and have always been one, you at least go through a process of consciously assimilating this fact. You begin to name what was previously unnameable for you, to explore in the joyous light of day what was previously perceived but dimly in the shadows.

One of the great advantages of this kind of process of conscious conversion is that you do not take the spiritual practices of your chosen path for granted, as one who grows up within a particular religious tradition may do. Those living in traditional societies or close-knit communities based on a single religion may maintain certain religious observances just because their families, friends, and neighbours do so. They may enjoy or find comfort in particular practices and traditions because they have been familiar since childhood, without necessarily considering their significance very fully. These possibilities are simply not open to the convert, who usually wants to know the point of any spiritual practice he or she undertakes: what are the benefits of it? How did it originate? Is it appropriate for me? We want to know the answers to these questions, especially if the practice does not have immediate appeal for us or requires a lot of effort – or perhaps just seems a bit puzzling.

Although we do not necessarily need to know how and why something works in order for it to have an effect, this spirit of enquiry is generally healthy and helpful in the spiritual life. We are likely to be more committed to spiritual practices and to make more effective use of them if we understand something of their meaning and function. None the less, like many positive mental attitudes, the desire to know all about what we are getting into has a 'near enemy', and one to which Westerners are often prone. The 'near enemy' is that attitude which holds that we can fully penetrate the significance of things through the intellect alone, that once we have thoroughly conceptualized something, we know all there is to know about it. A Buddhist, avowedly striving towards a direct knowledge of reality which goes beyond all concepts, should of course not fall into this way of thinking. And yet our conditioning by the Western tradition of scientific rationalism is strong and almost inevitably it provides the unspoken assumptions behind our trains of thought.

Another closet enemy of our quest for knowledge is the desire simply to have ready opinions on a given subject which we can contribute in conversation or repeat to ourselves when challenging questions arise. This desire leads us to pick up and hoard a myriad second-hand bits of information – and often misinformation – for later use, without really knowing much at all from personal experience, study, and reflection. One of the problems which Sangharakshita encountered on his return to England after twenty years in India was the enormous amount of misinformation about Buddhism that was circulating among British Buddhists in the 1960s. Much of the material in this book is based on lectures and seminars which Sangharakshita gave during the first few years after his return, when he was striving with great skill and tenacity to counteract the confusion and misunderstanding that were then prevalent.

There is much that can be explained about the origins and significance of Buddhist devotional practice, or puja. Sangharakshita expounds this material with his customary clarity and the authority that comes from an abundance of personal experience and study illuminated by deep reflection. But to read and understand all this is not in itself to know puja. Puja can only be known by practising it, experiencing it, being receptive to it over a considerable period of time, preferably practising it regularly and in community with others. Such experiential knowledge of puja cannot be handed to us on a plate. Even Sangharakshita can do no more within the covers of a book than hint at it and point us towards it. This volume is therefore a 'users' manual'. It is a companion to the practice of puja, not a substitute for it.

As a literary document, the book is an edited compilation of various teachings given by Sangharakshita on the subject of puja. The biggest single source, providing most of the material for chapters 5 and 7–12, and also some of the material for chapters 3 and 4, was the transcript of a seminar on the Sevenfold Puja led by Sangharakshita in 1978. Chapters 1 and 2 are drawn mainly from lectures given in 1967 and 1968 respectively, and a large part of chapter 13 comes from a lecture given in 1972. The remainder of the material comprises short extracts from numerous different seminars led by Sangharakshita, most of them held during the 1980s.

In order to make it more concise and readable, the seminar material has been rendered into continuous prose from the original dialogue format. The original transcription has been edited and in some places re-ordered quite substantially to make it more readable. Related pieces of material have been brought together and repetitions and points of merely passing interest omitted. Given that during the original seminars and lectures Sangharakshita was in part responding to specific questions asked and issues that were of particular concern to the Friends of the Western Buddhist Order (FWBO) at the time, it may be that in places the choice of material for discussion seems a little idiosyncratic. None the less, as long as it is of intrinsic interest and has relevance to puja, this material has been left in. In a few places material has been added that was not actually stated in the original seminar or lecture – perhaps being taken as read by those present – in order to complete a line of argument or to avoid a potential misunderstanding. The final edited version has of course been approved by Sangharakshita himself.

On behalf of the Spoken Word Project I gratefully acknowledge the work done by the many transcribers of Sangharakshita's spoken word material, under the direction of Dharmachari Silabhadra. Without their hard work, our own job would have been enormously more difficult.

Puja is a wonderfully joyful and effective form of spiritual practice. Sangharakshita's reflections on it provide us with a fascinating and inspiring mix of spiritual teaching, psychological insight, historical and cultural context, personal anecdote, and practical guidance, interlaced with gentle but compelling exhortation to practise the puja ever more deeply and authentically. This book has been compiled in the hope that its readers will be inspired and empowered to do just that.

Simon Carruth, Spoken Word Project, London, September 1995

1

EMOTIONAL ENERGY AND SPIRITUAL ASPIRATION

SOCRATES USED TO SAY that to know the good was sufficient. Doing the good, he said, would automatically follow from knowing it. This may have been true for Socrates, but it is certainly not true for the vast majority of us. For us, virtuous action by no means follows automatically upon knowledge of what is right. And why this should be so can be glimpsed in a criticism Aristotle levelled against Socrates. Socrates, he said, left altogether out of account what Aristotle called the 'irrational parts of the soul'.

The point at issue between these two philosophers of ancient Greece raises what is one of the basic problems of the spiritual life: the problem of how to translate knowing into being. To know and understand the truth, to gain an intuitive glimpse of the truth, is difficult enough, but to embody it in one's life and being is a hundred times more difficult. However much we may have understood, and however bright and clear that understanding may be, it is still very difficult indeed to put it into practice, to embody it in our day-to-day activities and behaviour. Any Buddhist will know this from experience.

Buddhism as a whole is very much concerned with this fundamental problem, and awareness of it underlies the distinction made in Buddhism between the path of vision and the path of transformation. The path of vision represents the initial spiritual insight or experience which starts a person off on the spiritual quest. For quite a number of people, this insight or experience comes spontaneously. It suddenly strikes them, even overwhelms them: an unaccountable glimpse of the truth, or at least of some higher and wider dimension of being and consciousness. For others the initial insight or experience may come as a result of study, perhaps while reading a book or musing upon some particular passage. It may come while trying to concentrate the mind during meditation. Indeed, it may come at any time and place, in any way, either spontaneously or in connection with some specific activity, whether religious in the formal sense or otherwise. And however it comes, it is what is known in Buddhism as the path of vision.

The path of transformation represents the gradual transformation of one's whole life in accordance with that initial vision. This second path is therefore very much longer and more difficult than the first. In the famous formulation of the Buddha's teaching known as the Noble Eight-fold Path, the path of vision is represented as the first step, which is best understood as 'perfect vision', although it is often translated, less help-fully, as 'right view' or 'right understanding'. The path of transformation is represented by all the other seven steps of the Eightfold Path: perfect emotion, perfect speech, perfect action, perfect livelihood, perfect effort, perfect awareness, and perfect *samādhi*.[1] These steps all represent the working out of the initial insight in different aspects of our life and activities.

But why should it be so difficult to translate knowing into being? Why are we not all like Socrates, able to know the good and immediately to do it without any hiatus between the two? What is it in us that prevents us from making the transition immediately from the path of vision to the path of transformation in its fullness? It is not difficult to answer this question. The answer is implicit in one of those popular figures of speech which sometimes embody a great deal of traditional wisdom. Suppose somebody is engaged in an undertaking which he knows he ought to be doing, but he does not apply himself to it very well and makes a poor job of it. In those circumstances we usually say 'His heart is not in it.'

His heart is not in it. In other words, he is not emotionally involved. Energy depends on emotion. If there is no emotion, there is no energy, no drive, and for that reason the work is not very well done. We can verify this point for ourselves from everyday experience. And if this is true of everyday life, it is perhaps even more true of the spiritual life. We may have a certain amount of spiritual insight, a certain amount of understanding, even a certain amount of experience. But if there is no emotional equivalent, as it were, of that understanding, it does not become embodied in our lives. A useful way of elucidating this situation is to think in terms of three different 'centres' from which we function: a thinking centre, an emotional centre, and a moving centre. (Within a specifically spiritual context these become 'higher centres': a higher thinking or even intuitive or visionary centre; a positive emotional centre; and a centre of spiritual practice and experience.) And what we find is that the thinking centre can only influence the moving centre through the emotional centre.

Understanding must pass through the emotions before it can influence the way we lead our lives. This is made clear by the structure of the Noble Eightfold Path. The first step is perfect vision. The second step, or aspect, is perfect emotion (traditionally translated 'right resolve'). Thus perfect emotion is the first of the seven steps which make up between them the path of transformation. Perfect vision has to pass through, be translated into, perfect emotion, before it can manifest as perfect speech, perfect action, and all the other successive steps of the path. The vital question is how to bring about this positive chain of causation. How do we involve our emotions in spiritual endeavour? And this in turn raises further questions. Why, one might ask, are the emotional energies not involved? Emotion is surely there in us somewhere – so what has happened to it? Why is it not readily available to us?

These questions can be answered both broadly and in more specific terms. Taking the broader issues first, we could say that if there is a general lack of free-flowing emotion in our society, it might be partly the result of necessary socialization. In civilized human society you can't just express your crude feelings and emotions. You might feel like murdering someone, but you can't just go and do it. You might feel like stealing something, but that doesn't mean you're at liberty to do so. A certain amount of socialization – a suppression of the cruder emotions – is necessary. Some of the emotions at work in, say, the behaviour of a football crowd just need to be suppressed in everyday society. The trouble is that this suppression may be carried to such an extreme that the greater part of people's emotional life is stifled – all the more so if their emotions are generally rather crude and unrefined. There may be nothing that can be allowed to get through.

In order to forestall the destructive expression of crude emotion, society conditions us to develop self-control. It is not an individual who is being crushed in most cases; individuality is not really there yet. Ultimately as

Buddhists we aim to be individuals – that is, to go beyond more or less unconsidered adherence to group values. But people need to be positive group members before they can develop individuality. Someone whose emotions are very crude and unruly can start refining them by becoming a positively functioning member of society, assuming that the society is a relatively positive one. If you are lucky with the sort of family you are born into and the sort of school you go to, you can emerge as a healthy group member and a potential individual, ready for the next step. But so many people are just like maimed animals, not even maimed human beings. A rampaging rebel is not necessarily a proto-individual.

So we must beware of romanticizing the situation. The football hooligan is not someone who is trying to be an individual. Very often he is just rejecting the necessary constraints even of the positive group, as if wanting to relapse into a state of animal anarchy and barbarism. It is not the case that, if the restrictions of society were removed, such a person would be revealed as a healthy individual. That would be the Rousseauist view: that the organization of society is wicked and oppresses the individual. There is indeed oppression, but what is being oppressed is not the individual. You need the socialization, the discipline, of the group to some extent before you can begin to be an individual. However, it is as though society insists on self-control to such a point that we get into the unconscious habit of it. It ceases to be conscious and becomes just an automatic process. We then cannot let go, even when occasionally society permits it, or when letting go feels a perfectly justifiable and positive thing to do. What happens only too often is that the incipient individual is crushed by too much control. As individuality starts to blossom, we need to move progressively from discipline, especially unconscious discipline, to genuine refinement of the emotions. An individual of high emotional development does not need external or even much internal discipline in order to behave in positive, helpful ways.

Refinement of the emotions – as opposed to control – can start to happen even in childhood, sometimes in connection with nature or maybe more often in connection with the arts. The child may experience something more refined and start enjoying, say, music or literature, though here obviously it depends on the kind of literature, the kind of music. Some types of music are palpably more refined than others. Young people dancing to rock music often appear to be in a daze, almost like robots – not lifted by any refinement of emotional experience, but immersed in a crude experience of movement and rhythm. There seems to be hardly any element of feeling in it at all, though it probably represents an advance on totally chaotic energy, inasmuch as it is rhythmical, which implies a measure of control. It is no doubt better to go to a rock concert than to throw beer bottles around and smash windows.

It is often assumed that living in large towns and cities makes it very difficult for us to stay in touch with our emotions. Certainly it can feel as though there is a lot of repression in cities, but there is also a lot of freedom. It can seem that people are 'out of touch with nature', but we have to be careful about jumping to conclusions. In the city you are after all still breathing air; you see the sky; there are at least some trees around. Does the average villager necessarily bother much about nature? I remember that once some Lepchas, up from the forest, passed my gate in Kalimpong. They looked up at the mountains and one of them said to the other, 'I can't understand why these foreign visitors keep looking at these mountains. What is there to see? Just some mountains.' They would have preferred Calcutta any day. So although city life may hold disadvantages for our emotional development, we must be very careful not to fall into 'back to the land' romanticism and bucolic cliché. Many people who live in the country regard the city as a place of liberation, away from the restrictions and narrowness, the pettiness and dogmatism, of the village.

The quality of one's contacts with people – the presence or absence of personal communication – is a major factor in this. As a rule, one's emotions are more likely to be blocked, and one's unblocked emotions are more likely to be negative, if one does not have satisfactory communication with other people. That is the basic criterion. And you can find opportunities for genuine communication whether you live in the village or in the city. Indeed, in the city you can always find like-minded people, whatever you are interested in. If you are interested in, say, painting, you can potentially find hundreds of other painters in the city, whereas in a village you might not find a single person to talk to about what matters most to you. But if you live in the city and you can't find any community of like-minded spirits, you can feel very lonely and isolated. The sort of human contact you have may not be at all satisfactory, and you may be conscious of this vast anonymous mass of people all around you, exerting a kind of psychic pressure – which is not a healthy situation. However, in the city there is at least the possibility of more intensive human contact than you would be likely to get in a small town or a village.

So we must beware of a generalized romantic Rousseauism or old-fashioned communism: the notion that people would be really good and happy and healthy and positive and friendly, if you only removed the social restrictions; if you only changed the political system; if you only took them out of the big evil cities and settled them down in some Utopia or some Eden. This view is simply not justified. Although Buddhism suggests that the right conditions will help people develop in a positive way, changes in external conditions are not always enough. You can meet some very negative people in what seem to be very positive surroundings. This is because, biologically speaking, we have an animal ancestry, we have animal instincts which are still very strong, indeed still stronger than anything else in us, in most cases. Civilization and culture form a very frail structure superimposed on what is virtually barbarism. We must be careful that in our attack on what is wrong in society, we do not move towards wanting to wipe out civilization and culture altogether, under the impression that there is a sort of primitive innocence underneath. In other words, the importance of the positive group should not be underestimated, however highly we value the spiritual community and however much the social group in which we find ourselves fails to live up to the ideals of a positive group. You can't go straight from primitive savagery into a spiritual community. The positive group is needed to socialize people's energies positively and constructively.

So this is a glimpse of the social background to the difficulty we sometimes experience in feeling and expressing our emotions – a difficulty which can stop us from putting our hearts into the spiritual life. Let us now move on to look more specifically at what happens to stop our emotions being fully involved, and what we can do to change the situation. In my view there are three main reasons why our emotions may not be available to us. They may be blocked; they may be wasted; or they may be too coarse.

Buddhist devotional ritual, or puja, is only one of many methods of spiritual practice which address the problem of how to engage our emotions with the spiritual life. Puja is concerned particularly with the third of the areas I have mentioned, that of refining emotional energies, although on occasions it may also have the effect of removing emotional blocks and preventing the waste of emotional energy, at least for the period that we are engaged in the puja. But an investigation of all three of these areas will help us to understand the special role of ritual in the spiritual life. After all, we can only refine energy that is available to us. If our emotions are blocked, if we habitually waste our emotional energies, we will have precious little energy upon which the puja can work its refining magic.

With regard to emotional energy that is blocked, Ouspensky, Gurdjieff's chief disciple, makes a rather striking point. In his book *In Search of the Miraculous*, he says that people are not nearly emotional enough. What he means by this is that our emotional centres are not functioning freely. The emotions do not flow readily; they have somehow got jammed. It is as though someone has thrown a spanner into the works, as perhaps they did when we were young. The English in particular are often said by people of other nationalities to be very reserved, and on the whole rather emotionally blocked. As a Russian, Ouspensky would probably have agreed with this view.

Whether or not it is true of the English that they are emotionally blocked as compared with other peoples, it is certainly true of adults as compared with the young. In children the emotional centre usually functions very freely indeed. Children are emotionally quite spontaneous, until their parents start conditioning them. Of course a child's emotional centre functions mostly in its lower aspects, but at least it functions freely and spontaneously. In adults this is usually not the case. Very often, the older people grow, the more they are emotionally blocked and unable to express themselves from the heart.

There are various reasons for this blockage. One is that for years on end we may be engaged in routine mechanical work, work into which we are unable to put our emotional energies, work in which we are simply not interested. The effort we have to put into this kind of work induces strain and difficulty, tension and worry. It causes unpleasant reactions and after-effects in us. Inasmuch as we cannot put our emotional energies into work, we get into the habit, as it were, of keeping them in reserve, until eventually those emotional energies become congealed. First they get sticky and gluey, then they harden within us more and more, and ultimately they even petrify, so that we are unable to put any vitality or enthusiasm at all into work or anything else.

Sometimes emotional blockage comes about through plain frustration and disappointment. Many people never really find any positive or creative outlet for their emotions in the course of their lives, whether through work or friendships or whatever. Some people again are very afraid of being wounded through their emotions, so they do not take the risk of letting their emotional energies flow out. They keep them to themselves.

The absence of any real communication with other people is another important cause of blocked emotions. It is quite possible to know many people, have many acquaintances, but never really to communicate with anybody. If we rarely get the opportunity for real communication, on occasions when we do chance to communicate fully with somebody, one result is a feeling of emotional liberation, as though energy has flowed out of us. But, paradoxically, we do not feel depleted by energy flowing out in this way – we feel all the more full of energy. Many people, however, never get the opportunity for this sort of communication. They may try to communicate but they come up against a sort of blank wall – there is no response – so again their emotional energy gets blocked, and they feel impoverished by the whole experience.

The wrong type of conditioning, especially the wrong type of religious conditioning, is also responsible for a great deal of stunted emotion. The orthodox Christian teaching about morals and particularly about sex is a prime example. Most Westerners have been subject to this at some time or other, usually when they were young.

The net effect of all these factors is that a great many people in the West today can be described as emotionally blocked. There is no free outward flow of emotional energy and so their lives are impoverished not only spiritually but even on the psychological level, the everyday human level.

Fortunately these emotional blockages can be removed. As a first step, we can develop greater self-knowledge. Of course, none of us like to think of ourselves as being emotionally blocked. We like to think that we are kind and friendly and outward-going and spontaneous. But in all likelihood the only way we are going to be these things is by first recognizing that we are nowhere near being them, that in fact we are – almost all of us – chronically blocked, so that we do not fully express the emotional drives within us. Uncomfortable though it may be, we have to face up to this fact. Furthermore, we need to try to understand why it is so – not in an intellectual way by reading books on psychology, but just by trying to see how it comes about in practice that our feelings do not find expression, that they go unrecognized, sometimes even by ourselves.

Sometimes emotional blockages are removed 'automatically' in the course of meditation. Even without our knowing anything about it, a release quite often happens in this way. That is why sometimes in the midst of a meditation someone will start crying, perhaps weeping bitterly: it is the relaxation, the resolution at least to some extent, of an emotional blockage. It is a very positive thing when it happens.

Some people find communication exercises very helpful. As practised in the FWBO, communication exercises involve two people sitting opposite each other. After 'just looking' at one another for a few minutes, one of them repeats some predetermined phrase (e.g. 'The sky is blue today') while the other responds with 'Yes', 'OK', or 'All right'. They then exchange roles and repeat this exercise, and finish with a further period of 'just looking'. The aim is to overcome social inhibitions to communication. At the end of such exercises, people often feel emotionally liberated, as though energy were pouring out of them. They feel greatly stimulated, much more vital and alive than before, because a portion of that blocked energy has been liberated. In these and many other ways previously blocked energy is made available to the whole of the conscious psyche.

Even if the emotions are not blocked, emotional energy may not be available because it is being wasted. We waste it all the time, by indulging in negative emotions such as fear, hatred, jealousy, self-pity, irrational guilt, anxiety, and so on. There is not a scrap of good in any of these negative emotions. They are completely useless and indeed positively harmful. But they fester in most people's minds most of the time. Not only do they fester; frequently they find outward verbal expressions which constantly drain away our emotional energy. No wonder we often feel so weak and depleted.

For example, some people grumble all the time. In Britain it is traditional to grumble about the weather. If it is raining, well, it ought not to be raining, regardless of how good the rain is for the farmer's crops. If it is hot, then of course it is too hot; but if it is cold, it is sure to be too cold. Making the weather into a whipping-boy for our unconscious negative emotions, we persist in grumbling about it. Some people grumble not only about the weather but about almost everything. Satisfied with nothing, they are in a state of constant disgruntlement. This is simply negative emotion finding an outlet.

Another common example of the kind of emotionally draining expression I am referring to is carping criticism. There are people who have a positive genius for finding fault. However good something may be, however successfully something has turned out, they always manage to discover something wrong with it. Nothing is quite satisfactory. Everything is somehow inadequate. Needless to say, I am not speaking here of objective, detached criticism, which is quite a different thing – and unfortunately very rare. Someone who habitually criticizes is inevitably expressing negative emotion.

The next 'verbal leak' I want to mention has no proper name in English, so I have taken the liberty of coining one: 'dismal-jimmyism'. During the second world war this was officially known as 'spreading alarm and despondency', and in those days it was a punishable offence. A dismal jimmy could be hauled up in front of the magistrate for spreading alarm and despondency. Perhaps it would be a good idea if it were still an offence. The dismal jimmy is always predicting disaster and exaggerating difficulties. He or she thinks that nothing is going to go right, assures you that you cannot possibly succeed, pours cold water on all your cherished schemes and plans. And even if you do succeed, such a person will usually shake his head gloomily and remark 'It would have been much better if you had failed.'

And there is a form of verbal expression which is even more harmful: gossip. Gossip is one of the most common expressions of negative emotion and also one of the most dangerous. It is very rarely innocent. It may start off innocently enough: 'What do you think about old so-and-so – how is he getting on?' But within half a minute we are up to our necks in tale-telling and insinuations of the worst possible kind. Spreading malicious gossip is really spreading poison within society. It is something which should be avoided at all costs.

Lastly, another all-too-familiar variety of negativity is nagging. This almost invariably happens between husband and wife, and there is a reason for that. If the nagger tried it on anybody else, that person would just leave straightaway, but husband and wife are tied to each other and cannot escape. Traditionally, of course, it is the wife who is cast in the role of the nagger but I rather suspect that the nagging husband is no less common. Nagging kept up – and some people keep it up for hours on end, day after day, week after week – is psychologically very damaging. To be a little provocative, I would go so far as to say that habitual nagging is much worse than occasional adultery.

So these are some of the commonest verbal expressions of negative emotion: grumbling, carping criticism, dismal-jimmyism, gossip, and nagging – a horrible collection. And the only thing to do about them is just to stop. If you start making excuses for them you are already giving in to them. So don't beat about the bush. One of the French poets is reported to have said: 'Take rhetoric and wring its neck.' We might say the same thing about these verbal excrescences: just take them and wring their necks. To do this of course means maintaining constant watchfulness over ourselves so that we do not involuntarily, out of sheer force of habit, start grumbling or gossiping or any of the rest. If we can just cut them off at the roots, a great deal of energy will be saved. And sometimes we will find that the best thing we can do is to say nothing at all.

Something which a lot of people notice on meditation retreats during which there are extended periods of silence is that they experience an access of energy. They feel more alive. This is partly because talking in itself takes effort but perhaps mainly because what we say is so often an expression of negative emotions which waste and drain away energy. For this reason silence is an extremely important spiritual discipline, whether in Buddhism, Hinduism, or Christianity. In all these great spiritual traditions silence is considered important, if not imperative, for the person who seeks to lead a spiritual life. In Pali and Sanskrit there is one word, *muni*, for both the man who is silent and the wise man. Of course, the 'wise man' who is silent is not silent because he is stupid or incommunicative. Nor does he experience discomfort when nothing is being said. He is never the person who feels the need to announce 'Isn't everybody quiet today!' So the silent person is very often the wise person, not least because he or she avoids wasting energy on negative verbiage.

The third reason why emotional energy is not available for the spiritual life is because it is too coarse. Higher thought, intuition, spiritual vision, can only act through the higher emotions. The ordinary positive emotions have therefore to be refined, sublimated. There are three principal ways to do this: first, through faith and devotion; second, through the fine arts; and third, perhaps most effectively, through a combination of these two.

Just allowing ourselves fully to experience and express whatever feelings we have of faith and devotion towards our spiritual ideal can be very beneficial. By faith and devotion I mean what in Buddhism is generally called *śraddhā*. This term is usually translated as 'faith' although it does not really mean that. The word *śraddhā* comes from a Sanskrit root meaning 'to place the heart on', and it represents our full emotional response to higher reality, to spiritual truth. It is important to understand the difference between *śraddhā* in the Buddhist sense and the kind of religious faith which has become discredited in the eyes of so many Westerners.

Faith occupies an important place in all traditional religions. The majority of the followers of these religions do not understand their religion in an intellectual sense, but none the less they have faith, they have devotion, and such faith gives the traditional religions their organizational – as distinct from their spiritual – strength. But unfortunately this faith is often not acted upon by the higher thinking centre, which remains more or less inactive. In other words popular faith and devotion are not generally linked to any higher spiritual vision or insight. They function under their own steam and decide their own course. More than that, it very often happens that the emotional centre itself tries to do the work of the higher thinking centre. The result is that instead of knowledge, there is merely belief. Belief eventually, inevitably, hardens into dogma; and dogma in time becomes quite irreconcilable with the intellect.

This has happened in the modern world, especially – in the case of religion in the West – with Christianity. That is why modern Western people usually react rather strongly against anything that smacks of faith or devotion. They are really reacting against the illegitimate functioning of faith and devotion, against the usurpation by the emotional centre of the function of the higher thinking centre. So it comes about that people may take to Buddhism, practise meditation, study the Dharma, and consider themselves Buddhists, but still have a resistance to faith and devotion, and everything connected with them. This theme will be explored further in chapter 2.

The second way of refining the emotional energies is through the fine arts: the enjoyment of poetry, music, especially classical music, painting, and so on. For many people nowadays this is the easiest, as well as the most natural and enjoyable, way of refining the emotional energies. I would go as far as to say that for many intelligent people one or another of the fine arts functions almost as a substitute for religion itself. People who would not dream of going to church may have no objection to going to hear, say, a concert performance of a mass by Bach or Mozart. The musical expression of devotional feelings appeals to them and they respond to it in a way they would find impossible within a formal religious framework.

Finally, the emotional energies can be refined by a combination of faith and devotion with one or more of the fine arts. Such a combination of devotion and poetry is what we encounter in such practices as the Sevenfold Puja.[2] The Sevenfold Puja is a devotional ritual in which we collectively evoke various spiritual emotions. And these emotions arise in response to our common ideals and shared vision of reality as represented by the Three Jewels – the Buddha, the Dharma, and the Sangha. In the case of the Sevenfold Puja we practise in the FWBO, this evocation is through verses selected from the very beautiful devotional poetry of the great sage Śāntideva.

The origins, meaning, and practice of the Sevenfold Puja are fully discussed, section by section, in chapters 3 to 13. But although those chapters seek to explain what can be explained, I would emphasize that it is only participation in the puja that can give us a real appreciation of its significance and its effects. When we ourselves celebrate the Sevenfold Puja, which combines faith and devotion with poetry and sometimes an element of visual beauty – and music in some Buddhist traditions, we find that our emotional energies are to some extent refined. When this happens, it becomes possible for the vision and insight of the higher thinking centre to act through these refined, sublimated emotional energies directly on the moving centre. In this way, the whole of life is completely transformed.

2

THE PSYCHOLOGY OF RITUAL

BEFORE LOOKING AT THE RITUAL of the Sevenfold Puja itself in detail, I
want to say something more about ritual in general. As I suggested in the
last chapter, there has been in recent times a considerable reaction against
anything that smacks of faith and devotion. This has been in part caused
by the fact that popular faith has been divorced from what I have termed
the 'higher thinking faculty' and so become unacceptable to the intellect,
bringing the whole notion of faith and devotion into disrepute, and along
with it the practice of ritual. But unfortunately it has to be said that the
rejection of faith, devotion, and ritual is for most people not the result of
their own earnest and searching intellectual endeavour. More often than
not it is just a received view, a part of their conditioning which has no
more intellectual legitimacy than the 'blind faith' which they look down
upon.

Before we reject ritual we should really think about what is meant by
it. What does ritual really signify? What is it really trying to achieve? It
tends to be taken for granted that ritual is a sort of outgrowth upon
religion. Some people have a very simplified picture of the history of
religion, imagining a pristine, simple, purely spiritual teaching at the
outset which in the course of a few centuries has degenerated and become
loaded down with a lot of unnecessary ritual and dogma, so that

periodically it must be purified of these things. People who think in this way see ritual not as really belonging to the essence of religion, but as something added on afterwards, something which they can very well do without – even something harmful.

Other people again regard ritual as a kind of socio-cultural habit surviving from primitive times. Vaguely imagining tribal communities dancing around a bonfire at night, perhaps waving their spears, they think that something of this kind represents the basic, primal form of ritual, and that remnants of this sort of thing survive even in modern life and in the higher religions. According to this view, dancing around the maypole and taking part in a mass are the same sort of thing.

These rather dismissive views of ritual are beginning to shift in some radical circles, but they remain prevalent even among Buddhists, especially in the West. Some Western Buddhists have even been under the strange impression that there is no ritual in Buddhism. Indeed this is one reason why some of them are attracted to Buddhism, or at least to what they think is Buddhism.

It is true that there are elevated states of consciousness in which the need for ritual is transcended, in which our spiritual aspiration is so intrinsic to our being and so refined that it expresses itself purely spiritually and mentally, leaving the physical plane behind. If those who avoid taking part in ritual have attained to such states, that is fine. But we must not confuse that sort of highly positive development with the far more common case of someone who is inhibited about ritual expression because of all sorts of fears and misunderstandings.

The traditional Eastern Buddhist approach starts with devotion. Buddhists who are unable even to observe the precepts,[3] let alone meditate or reflect on the Dharma, are at least able to attend a puja and offer flowers to the Buddha. However, in the West we tend to have to work our way towards devotional practices through meditation and study. The Protestant religion in particular has involved, from its beginnings, a devaluation of ritual, and in its more extreme forms, like Quakerism, has allowed people to profess the Christian faith without any expression of devotion whatsoever. It is of course necessary to resist easy emotional tricks. It may even be necessary sometimes to withdraw from devotional ritual for a while if one has problems with it. But it is unfortunate that in the West we like to think we have gone beyond ritual altogether.

I believe there are two main historical sources of our current devaluation of ritual. The first is to be found in classical rationalism and the second in early psychoanalysis. Rationalism, which goes back to the eighteenth century, tried to reduce religion to a matter of personal and social morality, abolishing anything supernatural, anything metaphysical, in fact anything very spiritual. In its early days, rationalism, as its very name suggests, was hostile to all non-rational elements. In the eighteenth and nineteenth centuries people knew nothing about the subconscious or the unconscious, so it was quite easy for the rationalists and the great thinkers of the Enlightenment period in France, England, and Germany to discount all the non-rational aspects of religion. They were especially opposed to such colourful elements as ritual and to any kind of religious dogma. We are still living to some extent with this heritage of rationalism and reductionism from the eighteenth century.

A much more recent influence on our thinking, dating from early in the twentieth century, has been psychoanalysis. It may seem a little odd that psychoanalysis should be concerned with ritual. In fact this interest arose from early psychoanalysts' studies of the behaviour of neurotic patients. It was discovered that some kinds of neurotics performed private rituals which in many cases had no connection with the patient's own religious beliefs and practices, but which none the less did seem to be in many ways similar to religious rituals. One very common example of this is the personal ritual of compulsive washing. Some neurotics have a compulsion to wash their hands every ten minutes – indeed they can be obsessive about all aspects of cleanliness and hygiene. The early psychoanalysts quickly saw that this patently neurotic personal ritual was similar to certain religious rituals, in particular those of purification which feature in nearly all religions. Having noticed the similarity, they concluded that religious ritual and neurotic ritual were very closely related.

Thus it was that the pioneers of psychoanalysis tended to dismiss all religious ritual whatsoever as compulsive and neurotic. Psychoanalysis in its early days was a very self-confident movement. In the first flush of early success it made some sweeping statements and drew some rash conclusions which later on it had to retract or modify, and this was one of them. As psychoanalytic thinking developed, luminaries such as Jung and Fromm came to be much more sympathetic to religious ritual than Freud had been.

There is another factor which has led to confusion about the Buddhist attitude towards ritual, especially in Britain. The first English translations of Buddhist texts from the Pali Canon were made in the late nineteenth century by scholars from the Protestant tradition of Christianity. At that time religious circles in England were ringing with what was known as the 'ritualist controversy' between the high church Anglicans of the

Oxford Movement, who sought to revive ritual in the Church of England, and the more extreme members of the evangelical wing of the church. Evangelical associations even went so far as to launch prosecutions against Romanizing clergy who tried to introduce rituals which were not, strictly speaking, authorized by the Book of Common Prayer (and thus by Parliament).

The Protestant Pali scholars of the time could not help being influenced by prevailing religious attitudes, and we find them reading into the Pali texts attitudes which are not actually there, and embodying those readings in their translations. For instance, the third of the ten fetters which chain us down to *saṃsāra* and prevent us from realizing nirvāṇa is what is known as *śīlavrata-parāmarśa*, and this was translated as 'dependence on rites and ceremonies'. In other words, the impression was given that, as regards rites and ceremonies, the Buddha adopted a Protestant, as distinct from a Catholic, attitude. However, if we look a little more closely at the original term, we find it does not really mean 'rites and ceremonies' at all. *Śīla* is simply ethical rules, as in *pañcaśīla*, meaning the five ethical precepts. *Śīlavrata* literally means 'vow' and it is a word that was applied to various Vedic religious observances in the days of the Buddha. *Parāmarśa* means dependence in the sense of clinging and attachment, and treating something as an end in itself rather than as a means to an end. So *śīlavrata-parāmarśa* means attachment to ethical rules and religious observances of whatever kind, considered as ends in themselves. It is treating these things as ends rather than as means to an end that constitutes the fetter. We may conclude that what the Buddha had in mind when he spoke of this third fetter was what we today would call irrational dependence on ritual and religious practice in general.

Ritual is an integral part of Buddhism, as it is of all other religions, and an integral part of every school of Buddhism, whether Tibetan, Zen, or Theravāda. Some people like to contrast Theravādin Buddhism and, say, Tibetan Buddhism in this respect, implying that there is no ritual in Theravāda whereas Tibetan Buddhism is full of it (with the assumption that ritual represents a degeneration). But this view is quite wrong. The Theravāda, like any other form of Buddhism, is highly ritualistic. I remember, for instance, that when I visited the Tooth Relic Temple at Kandy in Sri Lanka many years ago, there were elaborate rituals going on all morning in front of what is believed to be the Buddha's tooth. Zen, in China and Japan, is also highly ritualistic. In a Zen monastery they don't spend all their time meditating. There are all sorts of rituals to engage in: chanting of sūtras, recitation of mantras, and a good deal of bowing down. This might come as rather a shock to some Western Zen addicts.

This is not of course to say that there are no differences between the schools as regards the significance accorded to ritual. I would say that, in Tibetan Buddhism especially, the ritual is much more symbolically and spiritually significant. In Theravādin countries it tends to be more of the nature of ceremony than ritual proper; it is not so well integrated into the doctrinal tradition.

My main point is that we cannot get away from ritual in Buddhism, nor should we try to do so. Instead we should try to understand ritual and see what it really is. Erich Fromm, who first introduced the psycho-analytical distinction between rational and irrational ritual, gives an excellent definition of rational ritual as 'shared action, expressive of common strivings, rooted in common values'. Every word of this defini-tion is of import, and worth discussing in some detail.

First of all, ritual is 'shared action'. The fact that ritual is a kind of action is indicated by the traditional Buddhist word for ritual, *kriya*, which in fact means 'action' – being etymologically connected with the word *karma*, which means action in a more ethical and psychological sense. So *kriya* or ritual is something done, it is an action, and this fact should, if nothing else, remind us that religion, the spiritual life, is not just a matter of thought and feeling, but also of action: both moral action and ritual action. According to Buddhist tradition, human nature is threefold: body, speech, and mind together make up our total personality. Religion, which is concerned with our total personality, must cater for all three – and in order to involve the body, it must entail action.

Only too often in the West our approach to Buddhism is too one-sided. We pick and choose what we feel suits us, and the result is that part of us is simply never engaged in our practice. We may meditate and study, but if we miss out devotion and ritual, part of us is not involved. We need a Buddhist tradition in the West which provides not only for the head, not only for the heart, but even for the body and speech.

Ritual is not only action, but action that is shared, done together with other people. Here we come to an important difference between irra-tional, obsessive-compulsive ritual, and rational ritual. Neurotic ritual tends to isolate people. Like washing your hands every ten minutes, it is something done alone which does not bring the person doing it closer to others – quite the reverse. Rational ritual, however, tends to bring people together, and not just physically so. The sense of togetherness can also be, indeed should also be, spiritual. The performance of ritual action in company with others should celebrate a common spiritual attitude. For this reason a feeling of fellowship is essential, which means that ritual implies a spirit of *mettā* (loving-kindness) and solidarity. If this is present, a very powerful spiritual atmosphere can be created.

Fromm's definition goes on to say that rational ritual is 'expressive of common strivings'. Ritual expresses a striving. It is something we make the effort – certainly in Buddhism – to do ourselves. It is not something which is done for us, say by a priest. We don't just sit back and watch someone else conduct it for us. Ritual of that kind is a degeneration. Meaningful ritual is a matter of striving and exertion. It is part of the Buddhist practitioner's *sādhana*, or spiritual practice, or spiritual *exertion*. Ritual is not for the lazy person. Anyone who believes that ritual is a comfortable substitute for the more demanding methods of spiritual practice has not experienced it as it should be performed.

To be a good ritualist is at least as difficult as, say, giving a lecture, or meditating, if not more so. A good ritualist has to be very mindful. You have to say each phrase and do each action in the correct order, in the correct manner, and with the right emphasis, often doing several things at the same time. You need to have your wits about you.

Ritual also requires attention to detail – you need to see that there is water in the offering bowls, that there are incense sticks, that the candles are alight, that the flowers are properly arranged. For a complex ritual, an expert may be required. Once when I lived in Kalimpong, I invited Dhardo Rimpoche,[4] my friend and teacher, to perform a rather complex ritual and, as the custom is, all the offerings were to be placed ready on the shrine before his arrival. Usually my own Tibetan students and disciples made the preparations themselves, but on this occasion they were not satisfied with that. They did set up the elaborate offerings – lots of little lamps, tormas, and so on – on lots of little tables, but they then called in a lama to check it all before the Rimpoche arrived. The lama came and cast his eye over the arrangements. 'No. This should be there, that should be over here, these should be the other way round....' In about five minutes he had made the necessary adjustments and satisfied himself that everything was in order. So this is the kind of attention to detail required of a good ritualist.

Good ritual must not only be correctly done, it must also be beautiful. If it is not beautiful, it is not inspiring. So an aesthetic sense is essential. Hindus don't generally mind any amount of disorder and dirt in their temples, even while rituals are being conducted. I have seen temples littered with old bits of newspaper (used for wrapping offerings), remnants of coconuts (coconuts being a common offering), and heaps of long-deceased flowers trodden into the floor. But in a Buddhist temple or shrine-room everything is very beautifully arranged, clean and bright. This is true in Tibet, in Sri Lanka, indeed in all Buddhist countries. And Hindus themselves are the first to be impressed by it.

Perhaps most important, a good ritualist must understand the meaning of it all. It is no use being able to do the ritual mechanically, to go through all the right actions, without understanding what is really going on. That would be empty ritual.

Finally, I would say a good ritualist needs plenty of physical stamina. You may have to sit chanting for long periods, from time to time performing various ritual actions, and always maintaining graceful composure and appropriate hand-gestures or *mudras*. This takes considerable physical vigour.

Sometimes we in the West like to think that ritual is a sort of kindergarten stage of religion, something for beginners. But the Tibetans do not think like that. Tibetan tradition permits only the spiritually advanced to do lengthy and complex rituals. Certainly every Tibetan Buddhist has a form of ritual which he or she does. But it is only the Rimpoches and the more highly developed people in general who are sanctioned to enact very long and complicated rituals, because ordinary folk do not have the necessary mindfulness, understanding, and stamina.

Dhardo Rimpoche, who was well versed in Buddhist philosophy, an excellent organizer, and highly knowledgeable about Buddhist yoga, was also a very good ritualist. I often watched him for hours on end going through certain rituals, and I sometimes wondered how he was able to correlate it all. He would be chanting maybe for half an hour or an hour, ringing his bell and making offerings. Sometimes as he was chanting and got towards the end of his text, he would start folding the silken cover in which the book was wrapped in a very elaborate way, to make a particular pattern. And I noticed that as the last tinkle of the bell died away, and the last word of the ritual was recited, the last flower thrown – at that very moment, the last fold of the cloth would be put in place. It was all synchronized, effortlessly, so it seemed. It was harmonized like a piece of music and all the elements ended together, just at the right moment, like a closing cadence. His gestures or mudras, like those of many lamas, were very beautiful to watch. He had been trained in these skills for many years and was a perfect master of them.

Most of us will not develop our capacity for ritual to that degree, but none the less the ritual we perform at our own level should be something which we work at, and make as harmonious and expressive as we possibly can. It should involve striving – and not only our own striving, but a common striving. The implication of this important point is that the practice of ritual is possible only within a spiritual community. If you are just doing it on your own, it will not be ritual in the full sense. It may be a striving, but it will not be a common striving.

Ritual in the full sense does not just presuppose a common striving; it also *expresses* that common striving. This is the most important point of all: that ritual is an expression. To quote a further definition of Fromm's, ritual is 'a symbolic expression of thoughts and feelings by action'. So what exactly is meant by 'expression'? Essentially expression means bringing something out from within, even from the depths within. It is in order to express our depths that symbolic expression is necessary. Conceptual expression isn't enough. Conceptual expression brings something out only from the conscious level of our minds – and we have got to do more than that. We have got to plumb the depths beneath the conscious level, to contact the parts of our being to which myth and symbol speak. We could say, in fact, that ritual is like an acting out of symbol or myth. By expressing what is deep within our being, we externalize it, see it, make it something we can know. We can then begin to understand it and incorporate it into our conscious attitude. In this way our whole being will be enriched and integrated. Tension between the conscious and the unconscious will be reduced. We will become more whole.

Through ritual expression, not only do we externalize and make conscious our deep spiritual feelings; we also strengthen and intensify them. This touches on another reason why quite a lot of people feel hesitant about expressing themselves through ritual speech and action. They are simply not sure about the feelings themselves. Perhaps in the case of many of us our devotional feelings are still quite underdeveloped. It is a big step to put our trust in these feelings, to give them space to grow and to exert their influence on our conscious lives.

All of this is a matter of experience. By participating in ritual to any degree, we come to know it. It happens even within very simple devotional meetings when we recite the Sevenfold Puja – as long as we do it properly, with concentration. In ritual we create a very specific atmosphere. Just as meditation has its own atmosphere, which is very beautiful, just as a talk on the Dharma has its own very positive and happy ambience, so the Sevenfold Puja also has a distinctive atmosphere of its own which derives from what is brought up from the depths, external-ized, and made conscious.

This atmosphere can have a distinct and noticeable effect. At a Buddhist Society Summer School which I attended shortly after my return to England in 1964, I remember being rather surprised that, although there were many lectures on the programme – and also a little meditation – there was no provision for any sort of puja. So one day I suggested that we might try out a little ritual in the evening. At first this suggestion was not very well received. I was told that English Buddhists were right off ritual; they preferred the rational approach. So I said 'Well, never mind. Even if only five or six people want it, let's try it.' It was announced, therefore, that there would be a short and simple puja conducted by myself at nine o'clock that evening. In the event, instead of having five or six people, we had practically the whole Summer School, about a hundred and forty people. It was difficult to get them all into the room. They continued to come every night after that and seemed thoroughly to enjoy it. Many people remarked that a special atmosphere was created. Something special manifested, they knew not how, they knew not why. But it came from the depths and it created an altogether more meaningful and harmonious atmosphere.

Sometimes people are starved of this sort of thing. They get just the intellectual, conceptual approach: books, talks, ideas, philosophy, theory. It is an imbalance which is even encouraged in some places in the East. I've known Theravādin bhikkhus[5] apologize for pujas and say that they were only for lay people, unintellectual people. Intellectuals – and of course Westerners were supposed to be honorary intellectuals – didn't need them at all. What was important was the intellectual understanding of the Dharma. I've even heard Buddhist bhikkhus say 'Well, we bhikkhus don't do pujas ourselves.' But although the intellectual approach is no less necessary than the devotional or the imaginal approaches, sooner or later we must begin to engage the depths, the vast resources of energy which lie in the unconscious mind. We must begin to speak the language of myth, symbol, and image, and in this way integrate the unconscious with the conscious. And this is what ritual, among other things, helps us to do.

Lastly, in terms of Fromm's definition, ritual is 'rooted in common values'. Ritual is never just ritual. It is not self-contained. It issues from a whole religious philosophy, a system of beliefs and values. And broadly speaking, the more highly developed the religion is, the richer its ritual expression. The two most highly developed religions of the world are probably Buddhism and Christianity and these two are, at least in their dominant forms, highly ritualistic. In Christianity, the main forms, the Eastern Orthodox Church and the Roman Catholic Church, are both very ritualistic. And in the case of Buddhism, the Tibetan schools, Ch'an, Zen, and even the Theravāda all give an important place to ritual.

Having studied Fromm's definition of ritual, let us apply it to a simple example drawn from Buddhism: the ritual of Going for Refuge, which is very basic but also very important. First of all, it is an action. We say *Buddhaṁ saraṇaṁ gacchāmi, gacchāmi* meaning 'I go'. In the Pali and the Sanskrit, the verb comes out very powerfully because it comes at the end. It is often translated as 'I go for refuge to the Buddha', but a far more powerful translation is 'To the Buddha for refuge I go'. This stresses the fact that Going for Refuge is an action, an action of the whole being. We go for Refuge with body, speech, and mind. In the Tantric tradition it is not felt to be enough to go for Refuge mentally and verbally. You also go for Refuge physically, literally prostrating in front of the image. It is a threefold practice which involves the whole being.

Not only is it an action; it is a shared action, because we repeat the verses of Refuge together, in unison. In traditional Buddhist countries, the bhikkhu, or monk, recites first and the others recite after him. What emerges is almost a dialogue; an almost dramatic element is introduced. This emphasizes the fact that we are not just doing something in the same way as other individuals who happen to be there. We do it *with* them, with heart and mind and body.

Next, the Going for Refuge expresses a common striving, which is that we aspire to realize the common goal of nirvāṇa or Enlightenment. We all want to become like the Buddha. We all want to follow the path of the Dharma. We all want to help, and to receive help from, other members of the Sangha.

Finally, our strivings are rooted in common values, the values which permeate the whole body of the Buddha's teaching. The Going for Refuge is not something isolated in itself. It grows out of the whole teaching and tradition. If one were to expound the meaning of the Three Jewels to which we go for Refuge in full detail, such an exposition would incorporate the whole of Buddhism.

So Fromm's definition of ritual is readily applicable to the fundamental Buddhist practice of Going for Refuge, and it helps to give us some understanding of the psychology of ritual and some appreciation of its value. But the real way to appreciate the value of ritual is to practise it. Some people, as I have indicated, do find this difficult at first.

When I was in Kalimpong, an Englishman came to stay with me who was like this. He had come to me to study Buddhism, and he was very interested in Buddhist philosophy, but he had been brought up as a Protestant and was strongly against ritual. He would say to me 'I like Buddhism, I love the philosophy, I like the sūtras and all the rest of it, but I just can't stand all this bowing and scraping to the shrine.' I would put the Buddhist view on ritual to him and we had several discussions and arguments about it, but whenever I mentioned actually doing a ritual he would go very quiet. He would join in our morning and evening meditations, but he would not take part in the accompanying pujas. He wouldn't even put his hands together. None the less, he was evidently thinking it over, and one day he came dashing into my room and said 'Bhante, I've done it!' So I asked 'What do you mean? What have you done?' He said 'Believe it or not, I went into the shrine-room just now and I bowed down.' I replied 'Well, that's very good. How do you feel?' And he said: 'I feel quite different. I wouldn't have thought it would make such a difference as that, but I feel quite different for having done it.'

3

ORIGINS OF THE SEVENFOLD PUJA

SPEAKING VERY BROADLY, we could say that the essence of puja is thinking about the Buddha, occupying one's mind with the thought of the Buddha. This thought is not just cold and intellectual, but embraces the heartfelt ideal of Buddhahood. The Buddha is very vividly present in front of us, either in the form of a *rūpa*,[6] or Buddha image, or else visualized, imagined. All the devotional exercises, such as the offerings which take place within the puja, are forms of thinking about the Buddha. Through them, we open ourselves to the ideal of Buddhahood, become more sensitive to it, and are inspired by it. And this paves the way for our eventually breaking through into that higher spiritual dimension which we refer to as the *bodhicitta*.[7]

The Sevenfold Puja is a sequence of seven different devotional moods or aspirations, each of which is evoked by a few verses of traditional text. The verses in the particular version of the Sevenfold Puja used within the FWBO come from a much longer set of over a thousand verses called the *Bodhicaryāvatāra*, the 'Entry into the Path of Enlightenment'.[8] This is a highly poetic and devotional work giving guidance on the attitudes and ways of life which a Bodhisattva should adopt. It was written by the great Buddhist master Śāntideva, who lived in India in the eighth century CE. Śāntideva was remarkable in many ways: as a great thinker and metaphysician; as an ardent devotee of the Three Jewels, strong in faith and veneration; and as an outstanding poet. His extraordinary range of qualities make the *Bodhicaryāvatāra* a singularly inspiring and important work.

The tradition of the Sevenfold Puja has its origins in what I believe to be the highest ideal known to humankind: the Bodhisattva ideal. I have explained the origin of this sevenfold form of devotional practice in chapter 4 of *A Survey of Buddhism*, as follows:

> Strictly speaking, the Path of the Bodhisattva consists primarily in the practice of the Six (or Ten) Perfections (*pāramitās*), the successful accomplishment of which carries him through ten successive stages (*bhūmis*) of spiritual attainment. So great, however, is the discrepancy between our ability to understand a spiritual teaching and our power to practise it, that most of those who give theoretical assent to the superiority of the Secret Path are unprepared for the practice even of the first pāramitā. Between the life of worldly or of 'spiritual' individualism, on the one hand, and the Transcendental Path of the Bodhisattva on the other, the Mahāyāna therefore interpolates a number of observances, the purpose of which is to prepare the mind of the Bodhisattva – or rather, of the Bodhisattva-to-be – for the practice of the Six or Ten Perfections. Taking the Bodhisattva Path in its very widest sense, we find that, including these observances, it can be divided into three great stages.... (1) The preliminary devotional practices known collectively as *anuttara-pūjā* or Supreme Worship; (2) the rising of the Thought of Enlightenment (*bodhicitta-utpāda*), the making of a great Vow (*praṇidhāna*), and the receiving of an Assurance of Enlightenment (*vyākaraṇa*) from a living Buddha; (3) the four *caryās* or courses of conduct, the third and most important of which is the Practice of the Perfections (*pāramitā-caryā*)....
>
> By Supreme Worship is meant not only the adoption of a reverential attitude of mind, but the celebration by the aspirant to Bodhisattvahood of a sort of daily office. Our chief literary source for the details of this practice is the second chapter of Śāntideva's sublime canticle the *Bodhicaryāvatāra*, a work of the eighth century. The practice itself, however, was an ancient one. In fact, like many other observances, it was part of the enormous body of doctrines and methods which the Mahāyāna had inherited from the Hīnayāna and assimilated to its own tradition. Flowers, lights, and incense had been offered to the Buddha even during his lifetime; sins had been

confessed to him; Brahmā Sahampati had implored him to turn the Wheel of the Dharma. On the basis of occurrences of this kind the Hīnayāna framed a simple daily office which is still recited, in its Pali form, by both monks and laymen in Theravādin lands. Some of the formulae used are as old as Buddhism itself. The use of the term *anuttara*, unsurpassed or supreme, for the Mahāyāna office, was perhaps intended to suggest a comparison with its more rudimentary Hīnayāna original. As described by Śāntideva, Supreme Worship comprises: (1) obeisance (*vandanā*) and worship (*pūjā*); (2) Going for Refuge (*śaraṇā-gamana*); (3) confession of sins (*pāpa-deśanā*); (4) rejoicing in merit (*puṇyānumodanā*); and (6) transference of merits (*pariṇāmanā*) and self-surrender (*atmabhāvādi-parityāgaḥ*).[9]

The Sevenfold Puja is thus essentially a sort of lead-up to the arising of the bodhicitta incorporating all the main Buddhist observances in a progressive sequence. In the quotation above I spoke of a sixfold puja, the puja and vandanā sections sometimes being joined together as one. I have since thought it better to bring out the significant difference between them by separating them. Also, we now use slightly different translations of some of the terms.

I should explain how we come to have the verses in the particular form that we use. In the early 1960s I wanted to make a version of the Sevenfold Puja which I had described in *A Survey of Buddhism* – just a very short, simple Sevenfold Puja to introduce at the Hampstead Buddhist Vihara. Knowing that the *Bodhicaryāvatāra* was used for this purpose in Tibet, I considered the available translations. There was then only one complete English translation of it in print, by Marion L. Matics. I was aware, however, that another English translation had been made some years previously but never printed in full. It was made by a friend of mine in London, Mrs Adrienne Bennett, with whom I was in correspondence while I was in India. Using Mrs Bennett's version, I took the framework of the Sevenfold Puja, then extracted from chapters 2 and 3 of the *Bodhicaryāvatāra* a few verses under each of the seven headings (the puja, the vandanā, and so on), and in this way arrived at our present version, which has since been published in *The FWBO Puja Book*.

In chapters 5 to 12, I shall give the relevant verses in both Mrs Bennett's translation and Matics's translation, to facilitate a clear understanding of each verse. Mrs Bennett's translation certainly conveys the spirit of Śāntideva much better, and is far more poetic and rhythmical. In some cases Matics's translation makes the literal meaning a little clearer but when it comes to reading aloud, it does not flow nearly so well. Since I first selected the verses, further translations of the *Bodhicaryāvatāra* have been made, notably that by Stephen Batchelor from the Tibetan, which is quite widely used.

It is quite possible to compile a different Sevenfold Puja by selecting appropriate verses from other traditional texts. I have myself arranged verses from the *Sūtra of Golden Light* under the same seven headings, for use on special occasions.[10] This compilation, which has not yet been published, includes a very ample set of verses on confession – a major theme of the sūtra – so it can be used when one wishes to stress that particular practice.

The origins of the puja we use – who wrote it, who translated it, how, when, and why it was compiled, and so on – are of historical interest. But it is important to remember that these historical origins are not of any liturgical relevance. When we take part in the puja we should regard it as primordial, something that has always been like that, rather than something associated with particular names and dates. Ideally we should relate to the puja as a timeless process which is going on throughout the universe, practised by countless beings.

4

How to Approach the Sevenfold Puja

WE SAW IN THE LAST CHAPTER that this form of puja originated as a specific practice to help give rise to the bodhicitta, the Will to Enlightenment, and this is clearly the way to look at it if we have got as far in our spiritual lives as to be thinking about the bodhicitta. The puja is centred on the Buddha who embodies Enlightenment. If you have a very strong feeling for Enlightenment, or the embodiment of Enlightenment, this suggests that ultimately you would like to be like the Buddha yourself. And if you have a very strong urge to be like that, this urge will in time become tantamount to the arising of the bodhicitta. The puja can function as an aid to this process. To put it in slightly different terms, the puja can aid the gradual process whereby one eventually commits oneself wholeheartedly to the Buddha, Dharma, and Sangha – or, as we say, one goes for Refuge.

If you have not reached this stage yet, you may see the puja just as a practice which is more colourful, more emotionally engaging, than, say, doctrinal study. For you it may be a practice which helps you to restore your enthusiasm for Buddhism when you have become a bit dull or dry. This too is quite valid – to use puja as a sort of emotional sweetener.

People have sometimes asked me why we should bother with puja at all. Why not just stick with the other practices which Buddhism has to offer? I have already suggested some of the reasons, but my immediate personal response to such a question is, well, I like puja. I love the flowers, the lighted candles, and the chanting. I think it is wonderful. I don't think it will take me all the way to Enlightenment, but it is something helpful along the way which I really enjoy and I would rather not do without it.

So perhaps this is the first thing to say about how to approach the puja: just enjoy it. Enjoy the colour, the poetry, the fragrance of the incense. Don't do it out of a sense of obligation, as though there were some rule that said you have to attend the puja whether you like it or not. Those who do not take to it can opt out of it. On the other hand, one can take the attitude that as other people seem to be enjoying it, it might be worth attending a few times to see what happens – but in a spirit of interest and experimentation, not one of duty.

If you have a developing interest in Buddhism but you are not drawn to puja, even having tried it a number of times, this is not something to be worried about. You can practise meditation or engage in study. We are not all attracted to the same forms of practice. This is why within the FWBO we don't prescribe just one particular spiritual practice – just mantra chanting or just meditation – as some Buddhist schools do. We make available a whole range of Buddhist activities, anything that will help at least some people to grow and develop. It is important, especially in the early stages of following the Buddhist path, to latch on to which-ever form of practice seems most inspiring and helpful to you. Other aspects will develop later.

Having said that, if you have decided to make puja a part of your spiritual practice, it is important to take part in it regularly. It may be tempting to skip doing pujas at times when you are not feeling very bright or inspired, but you could adopt just the opposite attitude. If you really feel like doing the puja, it probably doesn't matter too much if you happen to miss it. But if you don't feel like doing it, it can be really beneficial to do it anyway. And sometimes when you don't feel in the mood and may think you are just going through the motions, you may be surprised to find you end up having a very positive experience. So regular practice is important, as long as it comes out of your own sense of commitment, not because you feel some sort of pressure from others.

For most people the Sevenfold Puja does take some getting used to. It is a bit like eating wholesome food, or changing to tea without sugar. When your palate has become vitiated by spicy, salty, or sugary flavours, wholesome food can seem bland and uninviting until you get used to it; but then food becomes much more satisfying. Likewise, once you have made the transition to a regular practice of the puja, it is a source of delight.

The puja is very much rooted in Indian tradition and it can take quite a long time to get a feel for the language and the cultural references. We may well need to find out something of the traditional background. Some years ago someone did try to get round this need by composing an English equivalent to the traditional verses, bringing in roses and daffodils and making it poetic in the English way. But, perhaps surprisingly, people felt quite uncomfortable with it, and it didn't really come off – though I am not suggesting that it could never be done. But in any case, once we have overcome the initial unfamiliarity, there is a value in feeling connected with Buddhist tradition through the puja.

Some people have difficulty with the poetry of the puja because they take the words too literally. They forget that it is poetry, and Indian poetry to boot – the Indians do go in for very flowery language. I have known people who objected strongly to the words 'I offer them lamps encrusted with jewels' because the lamps on their shrine did not happen to have any jewels on them. They considered that referring to jewelled lamps in these circumstances was a breach of the precept against false speech and they were therefore quite unable to recite the words. They could not understand that it was an imaginative offering, an offering in spirit. We must try to get in touch with the spirit of the words and not take it all too literally. Of course, to say that the language is poetical does not mean that the puja is some kind of fantasy. It is no fantasy, but a poetical invocation of real spiritual forces.

But even without taking the words literally, the lavishness and exuberance of some of the language in the puja can be hard to take for those who prefer more of a Zen approach. Both the austere approach and the lavish approach to spiritual beauty have their merits and we can learn to appreciate them both. But English people particularly tend to shy away from exuberance; maybe this is just something we have got to get over. A middle path is probably needed. One can aim to give the shrine-room a rich but simple beauty, with extra decorations on festival days. The verses of the puja contain some quite lavish turns of phrase, but we recite them in a straightforward way, which also adds an element of simplicity.

During the Sevenfold Puja we refer to spiritual beings, the Buddhas and Bodhisattvas. How we should understand these references can be another cause of difficulty. Do we view such beings as having an objective existence or not? Up to a certain point it needn't matter too much. We can view the Buddha as representing our own innate potential, if we wish, and view the Protectors as aspects of our own better self and so on – that is quite valid. But even when thinking in this way, we cannot exclude the objective altogether. Suppose we were to actualize our potential. What would happen? We would then be Buddhas, objectively. In which case it is reasonable to suppose that others have actualized their potential before us and become Buddhas – objectively existing Buddhas who can help us spiritually. But it is important to be clear that they are not helpers in the mundane sense. There is no value in praying to them for wealth and riches. That has no place in the puja. The Buddhas and Bodhisattvas can help us only if we open ourselves to their influence. So there is a subjective and an objective aspect to the puja. If it were all subjective – just comforting feelings and well-meaning thoughts in our own minds – without anything really objective, without Buddhas – it would not get us very far.

Ideally, the carrying out of the Sevenfold Puja should recapitulate, in a very concentrated, intense form, attitudes and moods which we are trying to cultivate all the time. This overall purpose should become clearer as we study these attitudes and moods one by one in subsequent chapters. It means that we should not leave our worship, salutation, Going for Refuge, and so on until we get round to reciting them in the Sevenfold Puja. We should be working on them all the time so that when we come together with other members of the spiritual community to recite the puja, we are simply experiencing them in a more intense form and in unison. The puja is a statement and enactment of what we are concerned with, devoted to, committed to, all the time. We are trying to direct all our energies, all our activities, towards Enlightenment, and the puja is a sort of microcosm of that, with the Buddha image representing the ideal which we are seeking to realize and towards which all our energies are directed. For people coming along to a puja who do not normally try to direct their thoughts and feelings in this way, obviously the Sevenfold Puja will not and cannot mean so much.

In making this kind of effort to direct our thoughts and feelings, we are giving ourselves to the Buddha. So the puja is essentially an act of giving, not of receiving – or at least we only receive from it to the extent that we are able to give ourselves to it. It is primarily an action and only incidentally an experience. To go along expecting a great emotional experience from the puja without being committed to the ideal of Enlightenment is to miss the point. We just have to offer ourselves. If there is a feedback in the form of some emotional experience, so much the better, but we should not see that as the purpose of the puja. If it does not come – if our experience of the puja is even quite dry – that is still all right. It is enough that we go into the shrine-room and express our devotion and reverence to the Buddha.

During the puja our orientation should always be towards the Buddha. If we are sincere and receptive, we know that it is all for the sake of the Buddha, even if that awareness is as yet only germinal. If we should feel that our appreciation of the puja may be merely aesthetic, if we seem to be in danger of enjoying it as no more than a rather pleasant and colourful event, the answer is simply to think more about the Buddha.

The Sevenfold Puja is the act not of a single person or of a group of people, but of the spiritual community. Now you might think that a spiritual community is necessarily a kind of group – and indeed, grammatically, it has to be treated as such. But in fact it is not any kind of collectivity at all. It is a number of individuals whose complete individuality is in no way diluted or compromised by their acting in harmony with one another, by their being in sympathy with one another, and – in the context of the puja – by their speaking in unison with one another. So when the spiritual community refers to itself, neither of the terms 'we' or 'I' answers adequately to the purpose. In the Sevenfold Puja within the FWBO we use the singular throughout, as Śāntideva does. As a balance to this, however, in another puja which is much used in the FWBO, the 'Short Puja', we employ the first person plural.

It is not that the puja cannot ever be done on one's own. Indeed you have got to feel devotion as an individual before you can really meaningfully join in with others. You can even practise 'mental puja', going through the puja silently as a form of meditation, visualizing the Buddha, the offerings, and so on. This is regarded as a higher level of practice which is possible only for those who have the necessary power of concentration and experience. Certain yogis and lamas have an absolute minimum of shrine equipment – perhaps just a picture hanging on the wall – because they create everything else mentally. In fact if you do the puja mentally it is possible to do it all on a much grander scale. You can visualize a thousand lamps and imagine yourself offering the whole universe, which you can hardly do concretely, however devoted you may be. Indeed, you can be completely carried away by devotional feeling in a way that is hardly possible when your sense consciousness is involved.

But mental puja is only possible for someone with a lot of experience of vocally and physically performed puja – and this primarily means 'communal' puja. Individual puja performed vocally and physically is a very different experience from doing it together with others. It is still of value, but it cannot be so full and rich an experience. For those who do sometimes perform the puja alone, it may be helpful at least to imagine the presence of the whole spiritual community, to feel a sense of connectedness with others who are Going for Refuge.

Given that the puja is essentially an expression of the devotion of the whole community, it is almost part of the definition of puja that everybody present on a particular occasion should join in. If there are new people present who do not want to join in, then of course they need not do so. But those who consider themselves Buddhists definitely should take part; otherwise a division within the spiritual community is created between those who are participating and those who are not.

It is quite reasonable to think of the puja as a devotional exercise, a means of strengthening our devotional 'muscles', a means of furthering our own spiritual development, but this is a slightly limited way of looking at it. There is a much greater dimension to the practice of performing the puja together, as a spiritual community. In some of the Mahāyāna sūtras there are vivid accounts of the Bodhisattvas all assembled around the Buddha and praising him with all sorts of beautiful hymns. Some Bodhisattvas even take a vow, we are told, that they will worship all the Buddhas in the universe. They spend millions of years, as it were, going from one part of the universe to another, worshipping all the Buddhas that exist. This is a typically Mahāyāna way of stressing the importance of devotion and worship, even for the most advanced Bodhisattvas. And we can regard the Sevenfold Puja as a reflection of that kind of Bodhisattva activity on a much lower level. Just as on the level of the *sambhogakāya* (i.e. Reality as perceived by Bodhisattvas on an archetypal or celestial level) there is the archetypal Buddha surrounded by all the great Bodhisattvas who are singing his praises, so in our own imperfect world there is the Buddha image surrounded by a much more lowly sangha, also praising the Buddha to the best of its abilities. The puja we perform at our Buddhist centre or during our retreat is a reflection of that cosmic puja which is eternally in progress. It is, if you like, a *nirmāṇakāya* puja, i.e. Reality perceived and worshipped from a mundane level.

Incidentally, we may, if we wish, bring this larger perspective on our practice of the puja to greater prominence by placing symbols of the *trikāya*, the three 'bodies' of the Buddha, on the shrine. The traditional symbol for the *dharmakāya* is either a crystal sphere (like a divinatory 'crystal ball') or a model of a stupa; for the *sambhogakāya* it is a volume of scripture; and for the *nirmāṇakāya*, a small Buddha image.

The verses of the puja are recited in call and response, which means that somebody present leads the puja. The person who does this should be whoever has the greatest depth of experience in the spiritual life. The leader shows the way, in a sense, and therefore the person who takes this role should be the one whose Going for Refuge is the most effective. This gives greater depth to the proceedings. When the leader says 'To the Buddha for Refuge I go', this statement will mean something different from what it means when the less experienced of those present say it. But they can be conscious of the leader Going for Refuge in a deeper sense than they are yet able to do, and may aspire to go for Refuge in that deeper way. The point is that if you lead a puja, you don't 'officiate', you don't 'guide', you don't stand to one side and lead people through their devotions. Nor are you 'the leader' in any fixed sense. You are simply doing the puja yourself, and others are simply following your lead.

Since the aim is to experience fully the distinctive spiritual mood of each section, we should be careful not to go through it too quickly. That is one reason why a bell or gong is struck at the end of each section. As well as marking the transition from one section to another, it also creates something of a pause.

All times of day are good for pujas. A puja is a good way of closing the day as long as you are not too tired to engage with it – and it is probably fair to say that if you're not too tired to engage with a late-night party, you shouldn't be too tired to engage with a puja. The morning, say after breakfast, is an excellent time for a puja. It will tend to be more vigorous than a late evening puja, just because you are more rested and fresh. Another good time is just as it gets dark, especially if you are in the country. In the city, of course, this may be the rush hour, so it may be too noisy. If you are a 'night person', or at least are not too tired and sleepy, a midnight puja or even a very early morning puja, just before dawn, can be wonderful. There is a very good atmosphere for a puja at around midnight and, say, between three and four o'clock. It is quite a different experience then, as long as you are awake enough and rested enough to be able to appreciate it.

The puja naturally leads into a meditative mood. One can meditate either before or after a puja; both have their merits. Puja is a good preparation for meditation because it gets your energy moving in the right direction, as it were. It enables you to let go of wandering thoughts, to be more integrated and ready to settle down into the meditation. Also, if you have the puja first, everyone can sit on to meditate for as long as they like. On the other hand, some people prefer to do the meditation first because then they will be more fully present for the puja.

Sound – both chanting and the accompanying music, if there is any – is a very important aspect of the Sevenfold Puja. In the next chapter we shall look in some detail at the role the senses play in the puja. Suffice it to say for now that whatever kind of chanting or music is used, it should be uplifting and should convey as far as possible a sense of supramundane beauty. There are certain kinds of music that just would not be suitable for use in the context of a puja, and even certain styles of chanting which would be quite inappropriate. We must be aware of the way in which we are chanting, being careful to avoid a forced or harsh tone. People sometimes chant in a harsh, forced way not because they do not have very good voices but simply because they are not in a positive frame of mind.

Some people with musical talents may want to make personal 'musical offerings' during the puja. However, it is difficult to do this in a way which fits well with the overall spirit of the puja. This is partly because the piece of music has usually been composed for some other reason and partly because, even though it may be intended as an offering, it is difficult to avoid the element of performance being introduced. These considerations apply regardless of the quality of the music or the feeling imparted by it.

There are of course appropriate religious uses of music. In a Christian context, in churches and cathedrals, the traditional music does not seem to detract from the overall effect intended, because it is meant for that purpose and because it is very rarely an individual performance. Even if only one person is performing, the performer is anonymous, so there is no element of theatricality. However, in a smaller gathering such as is usual in a Western Buddhist context at the present time, where everybody knows exactly who is playing or singing, it can become a bit of a performance by that person. This goes against the mood because the puja, by its very nature, is the act of the spiritual community as a whole.

A further difficulty is that in the West the musical offering is not likely to be truly oriented to the Buddha, as it might be in India. A musical rendering during a Hindu temple service is not meant for the audience. It is meant for the god and it is played in front of him, for him to 'hear'. The congregation only *over*hears it. However, since that is not the Western tradition, a Westerner probably cannot genuinely feel that he is performing for the Buddha, ignoring everybody else. He is most likely to feel that he is doing it for the other people present. Thus while the rest of the puja is oriented from the assembled company to the Buddha, the performance in the middle is oriented in the opposite direction, from the performer to the audience, which strikes rather a jarring note.

Admittedly the Tibetans have successfully incorporated music into their pujas, but it is a quite different kind of music from that normally heard in the West. Tibetan musical accompaniment to the puja has a primordial, archetypal power to it which we in the West are hardly likely to be able to develop in the foreseeable future. Russian Orthodox and some early Catholic church music have something of that archetypal power, but it would be no good ending up with anything like Protestant hymns or nineteenth-century choral works. The Christian liturgy was originally something that went on, as it were, on its own account; ideally it was a reflection of a heavenly liturgy being conducted by the angels and archangels. It didn't require either an audience or audience participation. But gradually the Christian churches – including even the Roman Catholic church – have become secularized. We Buddhists have to be careful not to go the same way. Just because the music of, say, Bach is very refined and profound and stirring doesn't mean that it is necessarily appropriate in a strictly devotional context.

Basically, it is a matter of distinguishing between the sort of personal emotional experience we have when we go to the opera, say, and the essentially sober, dry-eyed, and not impersonal but supra-personal emotions associated with devotion proper. Perhaps devotional feeling can only develop when surface emotions have subsided. You may even have to go through a period when you don't experience anything very much at all in the puja but just do it anyway.

If we use music at all in the puja we should think only in terms of a little discreet musical accompaniment to the chanting – an occasional thump on a drum or a sounding of cymbals. We need, particularly in the case of music, to be on our guard against trying to get out of the puja some kind of emotional experience that it is not designed to give. No doubt there is something very thrilling about a traditional Tibetan puja but we have to remember that it has been developed over several hundred years. There is little point for us in trying to reproduce what for the Tibetans is authentic but to us must necessarily be a lot of exotic effects. Better a dull puja that is authentic in the sense of expressing a genuine offering of ourselves to the Three Jewels than a jazzed-up puja in which we offer 'spiritual entertainment' *to* ourselves. No doubt in time we will develop all sorts of different pujas in association with specific Buddhas and Bodhisattvas. But any experimentation, musical or otherwise, should be an expression of devotion rather than boredom. In a way, there's no room for experimentation at all. There's just doing it better. That said, a more substantial musical item might fit in very well in the course of a festival, either before or after the puja.

Another notable aspect of traditional Tibetan puja is its length. The Sevenfold Puja is really just a basic framework, and it is certainly a good idea to hold really big pujas from time to time. But you will notice, if you do ever attend a traditional Tibetan puja, that it is broken up not only with all sorts of mantras and readings and verses and banging of drums and ringing of bells, but also with *light refreshments*. Tea is served every forty-five minutes – it's all part of the puja. In this spirit, if a really long puja is organized in a Western context, the organizer needs to be realistic about just how long everyone can keep going with any real enthusiasm.

On the other hand, even with a twenty-minute puja (with just the usual short reading after the sixth section), it is all too easy for the attention to wander – unless you are practising it with quite a small group. It is, that is to say, easy to forget that the puja is something *you* are doing, that however many people are present, you are not just part of a crowd.

As we have seen, when reciting and chanting the puja, we should primarily be entering into the spiritual mood, the spiritual emotion, represented by each section. When we take part in the puja, it works very much on an emotional and devotional level, rather than an intellectual one. But it is important at other times for us to study the text of the puja so that we can increase our understanding of what lies behind it and reflect on how we can bring the motivations expressed in the puja into play in our daily lives. The text is eminently worthy of study; indeed, study of the whole *Bodhicaryāvatāra* will help to enrich our understanding and experience of the puja. In the following chapters I shall be focusing on each of the seven sections of the puja in turn, looking both at the verses from the *Bodhicaryāvatāra* we recite and at Matics's translation of them. We will begin, as the Sevenfold Puja begins, with worship.

5

WORSHIP

With mandarava, blue lotus, and jasmine,
With all flowers pleasing and fragrant,
And with garlands skilfully woven,
I pay honour to the princes of the Sages,
So worthy of veneration.

I envelop them in clouds of incense,
Sweet and penetrating;
I make them offerings of food, hard and soft,
And pleasing kinds of liquids to drink.

I offer them lamps, encrusted with jewels,
Festooned with golden lotus.
On the paving, sprinkled with perfume,
I scatter handfuls of beautiful flowers.
(Bennett)

With the blossoms of the coral tree, the blue lotus, jasmine, and the like; with all perfumed and delightful flowers, I praise the most praiseworthy best of sages with beautifully formed garlands. I envelop them with clouds of incense, delighting the mind with

dense, expanding aromas; and I offer to them an offering of various
moist and dry foods and libations. I offer them jewel lamps placed in
rows on golden lotuses; and on mosaic pavements anointed with
perfume I scatter many pleasing flowers.
(Matics)

THE MOST OBVIOUS AND PERHAPS THE MOST IMPORTANT impression we
get from these opening verses is one of beauty – spiritual beauty. Even if
we knew nothing at all about the Dharma or about the Sevenfold Puja,
just hearing these verses in an open-minded, receptive way would convey that particular kind of beauty to us. Mundane, sensuous things are
mentioned – flowers, lamps, and jewels – but the overall impression is
surely one of spiritual, rather than worldly, beauty. And if that higher
beauty is the object, the corresponding subjective feeling, the natural
response to it, is one of faith and devotion.

We set the scene by evoking this sense of refined sensuous beauty. And
what we set the scene for is faith and devotion. The words of the puja
and everything connected with it should convey that sort of mood, that
sort of emotion, that sort of atmosphere. The shrine-room where the puja
takes place should always be kept looking beautiful, down to the last
detail. Throughout the Buddhist world, great importance is attached to
the shrine and the shrine-room: it must be clean, light, bright, and
beautiful. The focal point of the shrine, the Buddha image or *rūpa*, greatly
affects the overall impression. It is important to choose an image which
does not merely remind us of the Buddha – because after all we know it
is the Buddha – but which actually conveys something of the Buddha
nature, of Enlightenment, by its sheer aesthetic presence. A Buddha
image is not just a means of sparking off some mechanical devotional
reflex. It must be a work of art, an object of refined spiritual beauty – and
all the accessories likewise. For example, we must be sensitive to the
colour of the cloth we are using on the shrine. In Buddhist countries they
tend to use a lot of yellow and red in association with anything religious
or spiritual, but there is no rule about colour as long as the overall effect
is one of spiritual beauty.

Incidentally, the table or pedestal upon which the Buddha image is
placed should not really be referred to as the shrine. A shrine is simply a
place where a sacred image, or in some cases a sacred relic, is kept. Nor
should the raised focal point of a Buddhist shrine be called an altar. An
altar, strictly speaking, is a place or a table where sacrifice takes place.
Originally an animal, or in some early societies even a human being,
would be slaughtered, and in later times fruits and flowers would be

burned in offering. The focal point of a church is quite properly said to be an altar because Christ is regarded as a sacrifice, an innocent victim being offered up to God as an atonement for the sins of humanity. But in Buddhism there is no such sacrifice. The object of devotion, the Buddha image, is placed on a table or a stand purely for convenience. It is not an altar but merely an image table. If you prepare, or help to prepare, the shrine yourself this will help to put you in a proper devotional mood for the puja. And if you are involved in shrine preparation, it is good to spend as long as possible doing it. You can make it a real labour of love.

And just as the beauty and cleanliness of the shrine create the right physical setting for the puja, the words of this first section of the puja also set the scene by conveying an impression of spiritual beauty. In the presence of such beauty we readily feel uplifted, devotional. The opening verses strike a note of spiritual delight awakened by the experience of beauty and we enter a calm, happy, delighted state. It is not devotion in the strong, ardent sense – which perhaps comes later. The keynote of the first stage, when entering the shrine, seeing the image, the flowers, and the lamps, is just to think 'How beautiful!' and to feel uplifted.

As well as responding to the beauty of the shrine, we also respond to the atmosphere created by those present. So we must not leave ourselves out of the picture; we too are part of the decorations, as it were. And it is not only a question of our disposition or attitude. Turning up for a puja in a beautifully-kept shrine-room looking dirty and scruffy does not add to the devotional atmosphere of the occasion. In the matter of dress, at least, bhikkhus automatically look decorative because they are in beautiful coloured robes. Usually on Buddhist occasions in south-east Asia there are bhikkhus in their yellows, oranges, and saffrons, lay men more often than not in white, and lay women in all sorts of brightly coloured saris. The overall effect is very colourful and enlivening. I would encourage people in the West also to take some care over their appearance for pujas. Perhaps one could keep aside a particular outfit, dress, or robe for pujas, especially for pujas on festive occasions.

How we sit is also important. It is best from an aesthetic point of view if those who are participating in a puja sit in regular parallel rows, not just wherever they happen to find themselves. When we come together for the puja, we are more than a random collection of people. We are not just an audience. We are in fact part of the Three Jewels, at least symbolically. Just as the Buddha image made out of wood or stone or metal symbolizes the Buddha jewel, Enlightenment itself, and just as beautifully bound Buddhist texts placed on the shrine symbolize the Dharma jewel, so we, sitting there in flesh and blood, symbolize the Sangha jewel, the Āryasaṅgha. Even if we are not ourselves *āryas*, even if we have not ourselves attained to the noble company of those moving inexorably towards Enlightenment, we should still seek to symbolize this Aryasangha in the context of the puja.

Let us now consider the verses individually.

With mandarava, blue lotus, and jasmine.

For some reason Matics has rendered 'mandarava' as 'blossoms of the coral tree'. The mandarava is a flower which occurs in various sūtras and it is usually explained as a heavenly flower, one which does not grow on Earth. It is enormous, as big as a cart wheel, and bright golden in colour – a sort of celestial marigold of gigantic size which comes floating down from the heavens when the Buddha happens to give a particularly good discourse. So by saying 'mandarava' right at the beginning of the puja, you immediately create a sort of archetypal atmosphere. You are offering not just earthly flowers, but heavenly flowers. You also offer blue lotus and jasmine, both of which have a special kind of fragrance.

With all flowers pleasing and fragrant,
And with garlands skilfully woven,
I pay honour to the princes of the Sages,
So worthy of veneration.

Flowers are the most characteristic Buddhist offering of all, mainly because they are so beautiful, pleasing, as Śāntideva says, to both the eye and the sense of smell. Flowers common in India, such as the lotus, jasmine, and tuberose, are spectacularly beautiful and have very sweet scents. A quite extraordinary atmosphere of beauty and purity can be created by massed flower offerings.

Śāntideva also mentions garlands, which the Indians are very fond of offering to distinguished visitors and guests. Hindus also place garlands around the necks of images, though Buddhists do not usually do this with Buddha images. The words 'skilfully woven' (or even 'beautifully formed' as Matics has it) convey care and devotion. Someone has given a lot of time and attention to stringing these garlands.

Offering flowers and garlands of one kind or another is, however, just the beginning. Śāntideva mentions many other things to be offered: fruits, herbs, jewels, waters, mountains of jewels, forest-places, vines, trees, fragrant incenses, wish-fulfilling trees, trees of jewels, lakes adorned with lotuses, the endlessly fascinating cry of wild geese, harvests, crops of grain. He offers all these things and then he prepares a bath for the Buddhas and their sons. He offers songs, water-jars encrusted with jewels and filled with flowers, fragrant waters, garments, and ornaments. It is all rather lavish. When I was composing the FWBO's Sevenfold Puja, I trimmed it down so as not to overwhelm the Western Buddhist with too many offerings. The verses I selected mention just flowers, incense, lamps, food, drink, and perfume. Flowers, incense, and lamps are the three main offerings from the earliest days which occur in all forms of Buddhism. All the others seem to have been added later on.

I envelop them in clouds of incense,
Sweet and penetrating.

Or according to Matics:

I envelop them with clouds of incense, delighting the mind with dense, expanding aromas.

Incense, which is described here variously as 'delighting the mind' and as 'sweet and penetrating', is very widely used in puja, with the obvious purpose of involving one of our most influential senses to a calming and uplifting effect. We breathe in something beautiful which affects the mind through the senses. But how exactly does it work? The sense of smell is a rather strange thing. If, for instance, we are surrounded by unpleasant, even disgusting smells, that puts us into a mood of withdrawal. We want to get away from them and if we cannot do so, we may become angry. This may have biological roots, based on the need to keep people away from things which would have a bad effect on them. Most bad smells have got some connection with decay or death, with something rotten which would not be good to eat.

On the other hand, a delightful, pleasant, fragrant smell tends to put us into a mental state characterized by welcoming, openness, happiness, satisfaction, and joy. It is as if the fragrant smell is the olfactory equivalent of what we call beauty when referring to visual objects, though the sense of sight is more subtle than the sense of smell, which is relatively gross. Less conscious than sight, more direct, more bodily, more sensuous, it can produce an almost hormonal reaction. So when the sense of smell is aroused, it is as though the body as well as the mind is participating in the puja, thus helping to close one of the main routes by which we are distracted.

It is noticeable that if you burn a lot of incense it seems to set up a sort of vibration in the atmosphere after a while. Traditionally, in the East, incense-like fragrances are associated with the presence of the gods or *devas*. A Burmese friend I stayed with for six months in Kalimpong (he would probably have been the king of Burma had Burma still been a monarchy and not a republic) took this idea quite literally. When I knew him he was about sixty or so. He and his wife had a bungalow and I stayed in a second, smaller guest bungalow a little lower down the hill than theirs. They were great believers in the devas and he told me that his wife could see them. He could not see them himself, but whenever they appeared there was a distinctly perceptible fragrance, as avowed by traditional lore. He believed that the devas were particularly connected with the Burmese royal family and were at their service, as it were. According to him, they used to supply him and the Princess with money. The Princess used to do her puja and in the morning, when they lifted up the Buddha image, they would find bank notes underneath. (Their friends had rather more mundane explanations for this.)

My Burmese friend was very keen indeed that I should have some experience of the devas, which his wife told him were tiny in appearance and very bright, almost like fireflies. One evening he was talking about devas in his usual rather excitable way, and he said 'I'll get the Princess to send one down to you.' So I sat there and he was gone for about half an hour. While he was gone the strange thing was that I perceived a very strong scent of jasmine. I was quite sure of this – it was a very marked scent – and I was still thinking about it when he came rushing down and said 'Did you see the devas?' I replied 'No, I didn't see any devas, but I smelt a very strong jasmine-like scent.' He was delighted with this and said 'Yes, the devas have visited you. That is a sure sign.'

Make of this story what you please, but one quite persuasive interpretation of this sort of experience is to take the devas as representing highly skilful states of mind. The medieval expression 'the odour of sanctity' may mean, as some commentators have irreverently suggested, that Christian saints didn't wash; but alternatively it perhaps derives from the fact that skilful mental states tend to produce positive physical manifestations, some of which can be perceived in the form of fragrant scents. And conversely it does appear that certain fragrances, or combinations of fragrances, can help you into a meditative state. Particular incenses produce particular effects. For instance, when I was in India I used to favour Tibetan incense in the morning. It seemed very fresh and breezy, a sort of pine-like scent. In the evening I used the sweeter Indian varieties of incense. Instead of automatically burning any old joss-stick, it is worth noticing the particular effects that different kinds of incense have and using them accordingly. When you are feeling rather sluggish and dull, use an incense that has a stimulating, open-air effect – I would suggest a good rose incense. On the other hand, when feeling restless and excitable, use one which has a calming effect – but even then it should be refined, clear, and clean: a plain, inexpensive sandalwood, say, rather than a cheap benzene-based product. Through such awareness we can make the most effective use of these devotional accessories.

> I make them offerings of food, hard and soft,
> And pleasing kinds of liquids to drink.

'Hard and soft' – which may also be rendered as 'dry and moist' – is a common Indian classification of food, nothing especially Buddhistic. 'Moist' or 'soft' means rice, dal, and curries, and 'hard' means baked things like chapatis and sweets. So it simply means food in general, all kinds of food. Offering food and drink to the Buddha image suggests that you are treating it like a guest, as though it were a live human being. It is worth examining the background to this.

The puja – whether Buddhist or Hindu – has its cultural roots in the tradition of Indian hospitality, the observance of which is seen as a great virtue. Guests who turn up at someone's house, especially when they arrive unexpectedly, are supposed to be welcomed in a spirit of heartfelt generosity and attention to their needs. They have probably come on foot and their feet are dusty, so first you give them water for washing the feet. Then you give them water to drink, to quench their thirst. Next you greet them by putting beautiful garlands of flowers around their necks to refresh them with the sweet fragrance. You may light incense to keep away the mosquitoes, and you may also light a lamp if it is getting dark. Sometimes lamps are waved in front of guests as a sign of welcome. This waving of lamps, called *arati*, occupies quite an important place in modern Hindu puja and can be seen in any Hindu temple in the evening. They have a 'tree', as it is called, of lamps which is rotated in front of the image. Indian Buddhists do not usually do this – they simply offer lights – but in either case the origin is in the lamp which is lit when guests arrive – because for poor people this is something of a luxury. After lighting, or even waving, a lamp, the Indian host may sprinkle guests with perfume, and then of course will give them something to eat. If any of the women or girls in the house are skilled at music, they will be called upon to play, to entertain the guests.

In the West we do not really have this sort of tradition, although perhaps we used to, at least in Christian monasteries. The monks were instructed that they should regard a guest as Christ himself come to take shelter among them. But nowadays a guest is someone whom you invite and who turns up at the appointed hour for a meal. Some people just do not like guests, because they get in the way, especially if they turn up uninvited. The word for 'guest' in Sanskrit is *atithi*. *Tithi* is a division of time, like the hour, so *atithi* is one who doesn't come at any particular time. So a guest is not someone you invite for an appointed hour; the *atithi* is the untimely guest, the stranger who just turns up and to whom you are bound to give hospitality simply because he is a stranger and needs food, drink, and shelter. Because life is not so leisurely, not so spacious, as it was a few centuries ago, unexpected guests are now regarded as a disruption to our tightly-organized schedule. This is very different from the Indian tradition of feeling honoured to receive an uninvited guest. In fact in ancient India, in Hinduism, they carried this so far as to say that the only justification for the household life was that you were thereby enabled to give entertainment to guests. As Western Buddhists we have to start from scratch and build up our sense of hospitality. We may, for example, have to work a bit harder at welcoming newcomers – not just to our homes, but to our Buddhist centres as well.

And it is from the Indian style of hospitality that the seven or eight traditional offerings have arisen. They may all literally be placed on the shrine: water for washing the feet, water for drinking, flowers, incense, perfume, lamps, and food. The optional eighth offering, music, may be represented on the shrine by a little pair of cymbals. But more usually, the seven or eight offerings are represented by seven or eight bowls of water.

The making of these offerings, which were originally made in the context of Indian social life to an honoured guest, signifies an attitude of welcoming the Buddha into the world. The Buddha is the guest, the untimely one who comes unexpectedly into the world from some other dimension – the dimension of Enlightenment. So in a way this practice involves treating the image as a living person. But as this doesn't come easily to Westerners, it is probably best to keep the offerings simple. Indeed, if we have been brought up in the Christian tradition, our only experience of making offerings at all may be in the context of a 'harvest festival', when the first fruits – bunches of grapes, apples, sheaves of corn or loaves of bread – are offered.

In some forms of Buddhism (and also in Hinduism) the image is bathed, dressed, and decorated, then fed and taken on outings – even taken to meet other images. The Hindus are particularly keen on this:

they take their images to meet other gods and goddesses who then return their visits, each time processing ceremoniously through the streets. The images are put to bed at night and woken up in the morning with music. In fact Hindus almost play with their images as children play with dolls. And some Japanese Buddhists go so far as to bathe an image of the infant Buddha in warm, weak tea. While this might not strike a very devotional note for us, and might even seem rather absurd, it does help people to relate to the image directly, on a human level.

Some people draw the line at offering food and drink. In India I personally did not like such offerings because of the smells: in the midst of all the fragrant odours of flowers and incense, a spicy curry smell seemed quite out of place. This is not just cultural conditioning – it is because the grosser senses are stimulated in the wrong way, for instance causing the mouth to water, which is clearly not desirable. The Nepalese, I'm afraid, sometimes offer raw meat, which is even less appropriate. In my view nothing more gross than perfume should be brought into a puja; but for those who do want to give food, it is best to offer fruit. If, on the other hand, food and drink seem inappropriate, you can simply offer flowers, lights, and incense; or you can just think of the flowers as being the offering, the lights being there to illuminate, and the incense to create a pleasant atmosphere.

There is another Hindu tradition – also practised in some Mahāyāna Buddhist countries – of eating the food offerings afterwards, which means that the puja becomes an indirect way of producing a feast. Sometimes people say that out of devotion they want to offer the Buddha whatever they are going to eat themselves, but this can easily confuse things. People put more and more offerings in front of the image because then they get more and more afterwards in the form of what the Hindus call *prasad*. But the significance of the offerings is symbolical, and their symbolic value should not be compromised by their also having a mundane consumer value for the worshipper. Eating and devotion should be kept strictly separate. They are not traditionally associated in Buddhism, at least not in early Buddhism.

I offer them lamps, encrusted with jewels,
Festooned with golden lotus.

There are several reasons why we offer lamps, or light. Before electric lighting, if you had a puja in the evening, you would need lamps anyway. But more importantly light has a very profound and universal symbolical significance. Light is knowledge; light is wisdom; light is Enlightenment.

Furthermore, although we may have forgotten the fact in these days of electricity, candle-light is very beautiful. Traditionally the light offered was usually either candle-light or oil-lamp light: very soft, and golden-glowing. It has its own aesthetic value, as part of the beautiful scene. So to explain the presence of light in the puja, I think we need look no further than the archetypal significance of light and its intrinsic beauty, especially in its more natural forms. Personally I don't like to see modern temples lit up with harsh electric bulbs and fluorescent lighting, sometimes even with naked bulbs around the Buddha's halo. Perhaps they are an expression of devotion, but it is devotion of a rather vulgar and garish kind with no refinement, no spiritual sensibility.

The main offerings, then, are flowers, light, and incense. The flowers can be seen as representing the whole of nature, even the whole of life in a way; and because their lives are so short, they are a gentle reminder of impermanence. The light reminds us not only of the light of the sun in the sky, but also of the 'light' of Enlightenment. And the sweet smell of incense suggests the integration into the puja of even the more gross, physical aspects of our being. With the aid of these offerings the scene of the puja represents a heightened mode of existence – almost like a miniature Pure Land. Indeed, the impression of the Pure Land you get from descriptions in the Mahāyāna sūtras is as if a great puja were going on all the time. There is the Buddha, not just an image but the Buddha himself on a real lotus throne. Flowers are falling continuously from the sky, and garlands of flowers are being offered. People are seated all around and incense is burning. Chants are being raised and the Dharma is being preached. Life there is just one long puja, and what could be more delightful than that? So when we are engaged in puja, sitting in the shrine-room in front of the image, it should be a foretaste of the Pure Land, of Sukhavati itself. That is the spirit in which we should approach puja.

6

OFFERINGS

HAVING IMAGINED THE MAKING OF OFFERINGS during the verses of worship, we usually make physical offerings to the shrine in between the Worship section and the Salutation section, while a mantra is chanted in unison by everybody present. On most occasions the Avalokiteśvara mantra is chanted at this stage, but a different mantra can be used for specific occasions – for instance, the Śākyamuni mantra if the puja is to be dedicated especially to the Buddha Śākyamuni. There is a discussion of mantras in chapter 13.

If there are a lot of people at the puja, offerings may not be made at this point in the proceedings but at the end of the puja. This is simply because of the time it takes. In most shrine-rooms only two or three people can make offerings at once, so it can take a very long time with large numbers. The custom has grown in the FWBO that the person leading the puja makes his or her offering last. There is no fixed rule about this, but it does have the advantage of signalling the end of that particular stage of the proceedings.

You need not feel that you have to make an offering just because you are present at a puja. It is understood and accepted that you will make an offering if you feel like it and you need not do so otherwise. Nobody should do it for the sake of appearances. On the other hand, someone may take an individual decision to go up and make an offering even though he or she does not feel like doing so, in the hope that this ritual action will help to generate the corresponding feeling. This would not be going through the motions so much as acting out of a sense of spiritual discipline and allowing this to take precedence over one's present state of mind. In any case, there is no rule about whether one should make an offering on a particular occasion, nor about what one should offer. In the FWBO people usually offer incense, but there are many other traditional kinds of offerings that can be made as well or instead. Flowers are the most usual, after incense.

Sometimes people write down confessions of some unskilful act they have done or resolutions to change their behaviour in a particular way and offer these to the shrine, perhaps on a little paper scroll. This can be a good way to emphasize that the confession or resolution is being made not just to aid one's personal development but as a means of giving oneself to the Three Jewels. We do need to take care that our offerings are not too idiosyncratic and subjective. We may feel an urge to offer something which is of special symbolic – not to say psychotherapeutic – significance to us, but we need to consider the effect it will have on the overall atmosphere of the puja, which is an act of the spiritual community in unison. I would say that, in general, originality of offerings is quite out of place in communal pujas.

For example, someone might feel like offering some bones to the shrine, but that might be simply inappropriate. It is true that in the Vajrayāna tradition of practice there are occasions when representations of parts of the body are offered, to symbolize the dedication of the five senses to the task of attaining Enlightenment. The Tibetans like to do this in as concrete a way as possible: they have a little bowl – perhaps a skull cup – with a pair of ears, a tongue, a nose, and so on all modelled very realistically out of barley flour. If a puja is dedicated to a wrathful deity you may even have pieces of meat – real or modelled – as offerings. By contrast, in the case of a White Tārā Puja or Avalokiteśvara Puja, you are traditionally supposed to make predominantly white offerings. Something along these lines might be appropriate in a context where all those present had some understanding of the Vajrayāna approach and had been going into the significance of such offerings. But practices of this kind have to be taken seriously, not followed on the basis of a personal whim.

People have been known to make an offering to the shrine that was particularly meaningful to them, and then take the item away again after the puja, but this waters down the whole idea of offerings, which are a form of *dāna* or giving. The Buddhist tradition is quite unambiguously that an offering, once made, should not be taken back. Otherwise it would be like giving someone a box of chocolates and then taking it back to eat the chocolates yourself. Of course things can be lent to the shrine to beautify it, but that is not the same as making an offering, and you would not place the object on the shrine during the Offerings section of the puja. A clear distinction should be drawn between these two actions.

We usually have incense available in front of the shrine for people to make use of, although this is not really an offering in the strict sense because it has not been provided by the person who offers it. It would perhaps be better for people to bring their own offerings, so that they are truly and clearly giving. Some people do bring flowers, at least on special occasions, but in general people in the West seem rather reluctant to do this. Eastern Buddhists would not dream of offering something which had been provided for them. They remember to bring their own offerings, and if by chance they find themselves without one, they buy an offering from the monks. They may even buy something – in Tibet it is very often a scarf – that has been offered previously by someone else. We in the West should perhaps reflect on this, but equally we need not be too rigid about it. The offering is a symbolic act and the most important thing is that we should have the feeling of giving, whether or not we are literally doing so.

The Salutation section represents the paying of outward physical respect. It is not enough to keep our feelings of reverence in our minds. Whenever we have any strong inner feeling, we will naturally want to express it outwardly, because we have bodies as well as minds and hearts. To feel something totally means also to feel it physically. Obeisance, the bowing down alluded to in the verses, is the physical expression of the respect we feel for the ideal of Enlightenment.

There is little difference in meaning between the two translations. Notice at the beginning a bit of characteristically Indian exuberance: 'As many atoms as there are in the thousand million worlds, so many times I make reverent salutation.' Clearly it is not to be taken literally. It really means that your life should be one continuous salutation.

First of all it is the Three Jewels – the Buddha, the Dharma, and the Sangha – that are saluted. More specifically, reverent salutation is made to the Buddhas of the three eras – that is, of past, present, and future – together with the Dharma and the Spiritual Community. The three Buddhas who usually represent the Buddhas of the past, present, and future are Dīpaṅkara, Śākyamuni, and Maitreya respectively.[11] Śāntideva introduces all three, rather than just Śākyamuni, to give the Salutation a more cosmic perspective. Śāntideva is a Mahayanist, and one of the features which distinguish the Mahāyāna from the Hīnayāna is its wider, more universal vision. Lama Govinda makes the important point that the Mahāyāna's recognition of the plurality of Buddhas throughout time and space represents the fact that Enlightenment can be obtained whenever and wherever circumstances and conditions permit.[12] It suggests the universality of Enlightenment and the universality of the Buddha's teaching. It is therefore implicit in the words of the Salutation that we are saluting the Three Jewels not only as our ideal, but as a universal ideal.

The word 'Saddharma' in the penultimate line of the first verse simply means the true, the real, the good Dharma. This term also appears in the title of a very important Mahāyāna sūtra, the *Saddharma-puṇḍarīka*, which means the 'White Lotus of the True Dharma'.

Since the objects of our reverent salutation are the Three Jewels, which are also the objects to which we go for Refuge, in what way does the Salutation differ from the Going for Refuge which succeeds it? In what way, indeed, does the Salutation differ from the Worship which precedes it? In fact each of these sections does represent a distinct response to the ideal, and each builds upon the one before it. During the Worship we are confronted by the spiritual ideal. We take delight in it and express that delight, but we don't really do anything about it. We have not started thinking about our own relationship to it. The verses in the Worship section don't say anything about the Dharma or the Sangha, only about the Buddha. But when we come to make our salutation, we are recognizing that the ideal is something very much higher than we are. We see the gulf that exists between us and it, a gulf which we will have to cross if we want to realize that ideal. Then in the Going for Refuge it is as though we begin to close the gap. In the Worship we are not really conscious of the gap, in the Salutation we become conscious of it, and in the Going for Refuge we are determined to close it by treading the path leading from where we are to where the Buddha is. Broadly speaking, this would seem to be the main factor distinguishing between these three phases, and linking them in a series.

Suppose you are travelling and you see a beautiful mountain peak in the distance. You admire it for its beauty; you look up to it, enjoy it, and delight in it. This corresponds to worship. It does not occur to you at this stage that you could possibly climb that peak. Then you start to think: 'That mountain is so much higher than I am; to climb it would be very difficult.' Becoming aware of where you are in relation to the mountain in this way corresponds to the Salutation. And having absorbed that situation you decide: 'All right, none the less I am going to climb that mountain,' and you start walking towards it. That is Going for Refuge.

Another aspect of the distinction between worship and Going for Refuge in Buddhism is that it may be considered quite appropriate to worship things other than the Three Jewels, but it is always misguided to go for refuge to anything other than the Three Jewels. For example, people throughout history have worshipped certain natural objects. In the presence of, say, a particular tree or rock which seems, at least materially speaking, superior to them in some respect, they have not only empathized with that tree, but also looked up to it. Some have taken it further, imagining that there is a spirit living in the tree. The tree is the house of the tree spirit, and it is the tree spirit which is worshipped, and to which even offerings are made. This sort of thing is a feature of all animistic and pagan religions.

Buddhism does not reject this kind of response to natural phenomena. This used to confuse many early Western visitors to, say, Burma. The Burmese appeared to follow two different religions. One minute they would be worshipping various gods, and the next they would be worshipping the Buddha. So it was said that Burmese Buddhism was adulterated with animism, or that the Burmese were simply inconsistent – but this was completely to misunderstand the situation. There is no incompatibility between Buddhism and animism. They really go together, just as paganism and Buddhism do. Animism is considered quite healthy. I sometimes wish that in Britain we had more sacred rocks, trees, and groves. Unfortunately there are not many of these sacred sites left.

None the less, while Buddhism has nothing to say against worshipping hills, trees, or rocks, it does take exception to going for refuge to them. If we do that, we are taking nature as our highest value, expecting something from nature which it cannot give. The Buddhist path is a search for the Unconditioned and nature cannot give us that, even though it can manifest qualities which are worthy of reverence.

In a similar vein, Buddhists do not believe that it is wrong to worship the 'gods of the round'. These gods are more powerful beings than humans, existing on higher, subtler (though still mundane) planes, and they can perhaps help us in worldly matters. But they cannot help us on the path to Enlightenment, so we should not go for refuge to them. It is also quite normal for Buddhists (at least in the East) to worship their parents in the sense of paying them honour, respect, and gratitude. Again, however, we would not go for refuge to them, unless of course they happened to be Enlightened.

In this sense we *merely* worship them. The Buddha himself clearly distinguished those of his followers who worshipped him and went for Refuge to him as their teacher from those who *merely* worshipped him in the same way they would worship anyone charismatic, powerful, influential, and to be propitiated – as, in short, they would worship a cult figure. There is nothing wrong in worshipping cult figures either, as long as you don't go for refuge to them. The problem is that cult figures almost always call for an absolute commitment from their followers, incorporating them into a power structure and then exploiting them.

Incidentally the words 'puja' (worship) and 'vandanā' (salutation) are not always sharply distinguished from each other in the way that I have distinguished them, and this can be a source of confusion. The two terms are more or less interchangeable in Sanskrit, depending on context and usage. 'Vandanā' can mean no more than a distant, almost social salutation, and 'puja' is then the more heartfelt expression. However, within the FWBO we have adopted the usage outlined above.

I pay homage to all the shrines,
And places in which the Bodhisattvas have been.

We pay homage to the shrines – the *caityas* or stupas – because of their associations with the Buddha's life and even with his physical body. The same applies to 'places in which the Bodhisattvas have been'. In medieval India there were all sorts of stupas and *caityas* erected in places which were traditionally identified as where the Buddha, as a Bodhisattva in his previous lives, had committed various noble actions and practised the pāramitās.[13] There was one, for example, on the spot where the future Buddha was supposed to have sacrificed his body to a starving tigress.

Next we 'make profound obeisance to the Teachers', because they help us to practise the Dharma. They take the place of the Buddha, as it were, in our day-to-day lives. 'Those to whom respectful salutation is due' means any worthy persons who are following the spiritual path. Our salutation overflows to them too.

The salutation is expressed not just in words, but also in the act of bowing down. In the case of the Worship section, we are making offerings, or giving gifts, which does not necessarily imply that we regard the person to whom we give the gifts as superior to us. Gifts can be exchanged between equals. (Puja can also mean bowing down, but in this case it definitely means making offerings.) But when we bow down to someone, we are consciously recognizing that person as superior. This bowing down is referred to explicitly in the line 'I make profound obeisance to the Teachers'. Sometimes in more ceremonial pujas people make full prostrations at this point. More commonly, people bow down when making offerings between the Worship and Salutation sections.

In the East actual prostration before the image, or before monks or teachers, is very common. In the West we may need to experiment to see how far we can go in our own cultural context. It is not really a sufficient expression of devotion just to recite the words – there should be some appropriate action – but there are different ways of bowing down: the full-length prostration, the kneeling prostration, the semi-kneeling prostration, and the *añjali* salutation, the salutation with folded hands. Whilst the appropriate action depends partly on cultural context – what is natural in India may not seem suitable in the West – it depends more importantly on the feelings of the person doing it. Some Westerners may feel self-conscious about prostrating but in the East there are people who approach it with too little conscious feeling. They often do it in a mechanical way, without even thinking about it, just because it is the custom. I knew a French Buddhist nun who used to go through all the motions, but even as she was getting up from her knees she would be starting to tell her teachers what to do or complaining to them about this and that.

Sometimes there are constraints of space in the shrine-room. There may only be room for people to do ordinary salutations, or for one person to make prostrations on behalf of everybody present. But it is good to keep up the connection with tradition as far as possible. Where there is space, it can be left to people's individual feelings what kind of salutation they make. This is what happened in the Buddha's time. In some of the *suttas* we find the Buddha seated, about to give a talk, and people are gradually arriving. It is mentioned that some prostrate themselves full-length before the Buddha, others salute him from a distance, and others simply sit down without saluting. The Buddha is never reported as saying anything about this. He never said that people should salute him in any particular way; he just left it to them. So perhaps that is what we should do.

Some people (especially people experiencing a puja ceremony for the first time) react quite strongly to the practice of prostrations. They may think it expresses a slavish mentality. Indeed, people can be outraged by what seems to them to be excessive respect paid either to images or to other human beings. This is an attitude which has deep roots in Western civilization, as is illustrated by the respective attitudes of the ancient Greeks and the ancient Persians. Apparently, when the two cultures came into contact with each other, one of the things which really shocked and displeased the Greeks was the Persians' custom of prostrating in front of their kings. The Greeks thought this most unbefitting a human being: humans should salute only the gods, and even the gods they should salute in quite a moderate fashion. After Alexander the Great became king of Persia, he upset some of his Greek followers by insisting they pay him respect in the manner of the Persians. The bluff, hearty Macedonians did not like that at all and thought that Alexander was getting a bit above himself. So this suspicion of prostration is not only found in the modern West. It goes right back to the ancient Greeks and is connected with their humanism, their respect for the individual – beginning with themselves.

I recall that during the first few weeks of my time in Kalimpong, when I was staying at the Dharmodaya Vihara, a visiting Christian priest stayed there for a few days. He was shocked and horrified by the respect which the Newar Buddhists paid to me as a novice monk, and said 'In the Catholic Church we don't even pay that sort of respect to the Pope.' Which may well be the case today, but as late as the last century it was still the custom to kiss the Pope's toe when one had an audience with him. He used to stick his toe out for the purpose.

So in view of the associations it has, we should be a little careful about prostration, and give consideration not only to our own devotional feelings but also to the susceptibilities of others who may be present. None the less, some form of physical salutation is important if we are to engage our emotions fully with this section and move forward from the stage of worship.

8

GOING FOR REFUGE

This very day
I go for my refuge
To the powerful protectors,
Whose purpose is to guard the universe;
The mighty conquerors who overcome suffering everywhere.

Wholeheartedly also I take my refuge
In the Dharma they have ascertained,
Which is the abode of security against the rounds of rebirth.
Likewise in the host of Bodhisattvas
I take my refuge.
(Bennett)

Therefore, I go now for refuge to the Lords of the earth, the ones labouring for the sake of the earth's protection, the Conquerors who dispel all fear; and likewise I go for refuge to the Dharma that is mastered by them, which consumes the fear of rebirth: and I go to the company of Bodhisattvas.
(Matics)

First we go for Refuge to 'the powerful protectors whose purpose is to guard the universe'. There is a possibility of misunderstanding in connection with this phrase, in that it might seem to suggest something like a creator deity. In fact the sense in which the Buddhas are said to be 'protectors' is not that they 'guard the universe' in the way that Christians would tell us God is supposed to, or protect us from worldly disasters in the way that God might, if he so wished. It is that they keep open the way to Enlightenment. The clue is perhaps to be found in the next two lines, in the fact that the Buddhas are called Jinas, or 'conquerors'. They overcome suffering everywhere by overcoming their own unskilful states, and inspiring and teaching others to overcome *their* unskilful mental states through their own efforts. We do not go for Refuge to the Buddha for protection from worldly calamities.

The Buddha, in other words, is not a god, though it would probably be impossible to erase this notion completely from the popular mind. The Hindus, especially the Bengalis, often call him 'Buddhadeva', and even some Buddhists worship him as though he were a god. I met with a striking example of this kind of confusion when I was on tour in Assam and staying with some Bengali Buddhists. There was to be a little puja, as is the custom, and they put a small Buddha image on the table and next to that an image of the Hindu goddess Lakshmi. I was quite surprised to find them worshipping this figure, but clearly they were expecting me to do some Buddha puja and some Lakshmi puja before I had my meal. Initially I was unsure what to do – it was not a situation I had run into before – but in the end I resolved it by quietly putting the Lakshmi image to one side so that she was not in the way of the puja. I didn't say anything, but I dare say they understood.

Moving on to the Dharma refuge, Matics's translation, 'the Dharma that is mastered by them', is probably more literal than Mrs Bennett's 'the Dharma they have ascertained'. None the less 'ascertained' is a very suitable term here. It means 'to find out or to assure oneself of the truth by experiencing it', and it avoids any inappropriate suggestion of power and control which may be implied by the term 'mastered'.

The Dharma – here meaning the transcendental Dharma – is described as 'the abode of security against the rounds of rebirth'. Someone who is on the Transcendental Path (i.e. someone who has gained some real insight into the nature of Reality) is secure against the rounds of rebirth and cannot fall into them any more, or at least not more than a certain number of times. This is what is meant by being secure.

In the case of the third refuge, the Sangha, notice that refuge is taken in 'the host of Bodhisattvas' – not just in a particular Bodhisattva but in the Aryasangha as a whole. Here 'Bodhisattvas' should be understood in the wider sense to include Stream-entrants (those whose future spiritual progress is assured) and Arhants (in Hīnayāna terms those who are fully Enlightened and will not be reborn again). These are sometimes called 'Hīnayāna Bodhisattvas'. We could call them 'incipient Bodhisattvas' in the sense that they could become Bodhisattvas if they woke up to that possibility.

There can be considerable confusion over the idea that there are two paths, one for the Bodhisattva and one for the Arhant. There was even a difference of opinion among Buddhists themselves in medieval times. Some would say that once people are on the Hīnayāna path, they can't retrace their steps: they go along that path, as it were to the bitter end. Having become a Stream-entrant, the only way forward is to become a Once-returner, a Non-returner, and finally an Arhant. But other authorities would say that it is possible to change paths. Someone following the Hīnayāna, having come on to the Transcendental Path as, say, a Stream-entrant, could, having become aware of the greater Mahāyāna ideal, decide thereafter to follow the Bodhisattva path. It seems to me that the root of the confusion is that the Arhant path, and perhaps also the Bodhisattva path, have been defined too narrowly and rigidly, making it difficult to bring the two together. The mistake – if one can speak in these terms – lay in separating them in that mutually exclusive way in the first place, rather than recognizing that the so-called 'Arhant path' and 'Bodhisattva path' represented different dimensions of what is essentially one and the same path.

Historically speaking, it is quite incorrect to represent the Buddha as teaching the 'Hīnayāna path'. The Buddha just taught the path or the way, and that was narrowed down by some of his followers into what became the Hīnayāna or Arhant path. The Mahayanists then had to broaden it out, but unfortunately the broadened version remained in contradistinction to the earlier, narrower version, and therefore it too had a certain limitation. I don't feel happy to talk in terms of separate Arhant and Bodhisattva paths at all, even though a lot of the surviving Buddhist canonical literature does just that. Such a separation does not seem to be borne out by the spiritual facts of the situation. It may well be that at certain stages of your spiritual career you are more aware of the individual aspect of the spiritual life while at other times you are more aware of the altruistic aspect, and you act accordingly. But eventually you must come to a state in which your mental constructions of subject and object, self and other, in their mutually exclusive sense, lose their significance. And surely from such a standpoint you will no longer distinguish between the Arhant ideal and the Bodhisattva ideal. Taking this view, we can adopt the position of the *Saddharma-puṇḍarīka Sūtra* and say that all three *yānas* or 'ways' merge into one *yāna*. The sūtra teaches that the Śrāvakayāna (the way of the disciple), the Pratyekabuddhayāna (the way of private or merely personal Enlightenment) and the Bodhisattvayāna (the way of the Bodhisattva) all merge into the Buddhayāna (the way of the Buddha). We can go even further and envisage the Hīnayāna, the Mahāyāna, and the Vajrayāna merging into one yāna, one path, one Dharma.

So questions such as whether an Arhant can wake up to the Bodhisattva ideal are quite artificial from a spiritual point of view. It is just a matter of reconciling different scholastic formulations. Sometimes this can be difficult, because the formulations themselves are one-sided, even mutually exclusive, but we should try to see ourselves simply as on the path of being a Buddhist, on the path to Enlightenment. The teachings which are found under the label 'Hīnayāna' certainly help us, and so do those found under the label 'Mahāyāna'. We can't afford to neglect either of them; they are not mutually exclusive paths between which we have to make a choice, but represent different emphases on different aspects of the spiritual life. A particular emphasis may be more relevant to our needs at one stage of our spiritual career than at another.

When we go for Refuge to the Dharma and to the Sangha, therefore, we should acknowledge them as being manifested in all three traditional yānas of Buddhism, rather than taking a narrow, sectarian view. In a similar way, when we go for Refuge to the Buddha-jewel, we should acknowledge it as being manifested in the Buddha's historical life, in his archetypal forms, and ultimately in his absolute nature, about which words are powerless to inform us.

Immediately after the Going for Refuge verses we recite the Five Precepts or, if only Order members, i.e. Dharmacharis or Dharmacharinis (literally 'Dharma-farers'), are present, the Ten Precepts. The recitation of the precepts at this stage underlines the fact that by virtue of our Going for Refuge we are committed to transforming our lives. Each precept has a negative form, in which we undertake to abstain from a particular kind of unskilful act, and also a positive form, in which we undertake to practise the corresponding skilful form of action. We normally recite the negative formulation of the precepts in Pali and the positive formulation in English. For the sake of clarity I shall give them all in English, but with the Pali terms for the various activities to be abstained from in brackets at the end of the negative precepts. The negative formulations of the Five Precepts may be rendered as follows:

I undertake to abstain from taking life (*pāṇātipātā*).
I undertake to abstain from taking the not-given (*adinnādānā*).
I undertake to abstain from sexual misconduct (*kāmesu micchācārā*).
I undertake to abstain from false speech (*musāvādā*).
I undertake to abstain from taking intoxicants (*surāmeraya majja pamādaṭṭhānā*).

The positive formulations are:

With deeds of loving kindness, I purify my body.
With open-handed generosity, I purify my body.
With stillness, simplicity, and contentment, I purify my body.
With truthful communication, I purify my speech.
With mindfulness clear and radiant, I purify my mind.

The negative formulations of the Ten Precepts are:

I undertake to abstain from taking life (*pāṇatipātā*).
I undertake to abstain from taking the not-given (*adinnādānā*).
I undertake to abstain from sexual misconduct (*kāmesu micchācārā*).
I undertake to abstain from false speech (*musāvādā*).
I undertake to abstain from harsh speech (*pharusavācā*).
I undertake to abstain from useless speech (*samphappalāpavācā*).
I undertake to abstain from slanderous speech (*pisuṇavācā*).
I undertake to abstain from covetousness (*abhijjhā*).
I undertake to abstain from animosity (*byāpādā*).
I undertake to abstain from false views (*micchādassanā*).

Their positive formulations are:

With deeds of loving kindness, I purify my body.
With open-handed generosity, I purify my body.
With stillness, simplicity, and contentment, I purify my body.
With truthful communication, I purify my speech.
With words kindly and gracious, I purify my speech.
With utterance helpful and harmonious, I purify my speech.
Abandoning covetousness for tranquillity, I purify my mind.
Changing hatred into compassion, I purify my mind.
Transforming ignorance into wisdom, I purify my mind.

Only nine items appear in the positive list because the sixth item is in fact two precepts rolled into one, corresponding to both the sixth and the seventh precepts in the negative list.

The difference between the Five Precepts and the Ten Precepts is not a matter of more or less of the same sort of thing. It is quite fundamental. For instance, if you were really to give up *micchādassanā*, or false views (the tenth precept), you would have attained at least Stream-entry – i.e. you would have achieved transcendental insight. Undertaking to eradicate *micchādassanā* suggests a commitment to the path of vision. Abstention from *abhijjhā* (covetousness) and *byāpādā* (hatred) means a commitment to the path of transformation. So these three precepts are not just precepts in the ethical sense like the others; they have a transcendental significance. They are oriented in the direction of Insight and Wisdom, so their significance goes far beyond the social and cultural level represented by the Five Precepts. This is why the Ten Precepts are taken by the Dharmachari or Dharmacharini. To go for Refuge effectively, you must intend, consciously and deliberately, to aim for the transcendental. Observing just the Five Precepts will only get you as far as a good rebirth. If you are seriously Going for Refuge, you want something much more than a good rebirth – you want Enlightenment – so you will need to take the last three of the Ten Precepts, which indicate purification of mind. It is not enough to purify your actions. It is not enough to purify your speech. You have got to purify your mind of ignorance, because only by doing so can you gain Enlightenment. Even though it is traditional in Buddhist countries for people to take the Three Refuges and Five Precepts and to consider themselves Buddhists because they do so, that is not really enough. It does not bring out the full significance of Going for Refuge in a Buddhist's personal life, practice, and experience.

Another major feature of the Ten Precepts is that the precept of *musāvādā*, false speech, is expanded into four precepts. This is highly significant. One could just as well have expanded some of the other precepts in this way, but speech has been singled out, emphasizing the tremendous importance of communication in the spiritual life. If you truly observe these precepts, you do not just speak *about* Going for Refuge; your speech *is* Going for Refuge. The medium is the message.

There is one more significant point to notice about the Ten Precepts. The fifth of the Five Precepts is missed out. There is a spiritual reason for this. The positive quality corresponding to this precept is awareness; one could say that the state of intoxication, partial or complete, represents a very gross form of unawareness. The mental states refrained from in the

Ten Precepts – *abhijjhā*, *byāpādā*, and *micchādassanā* – represent the more subtle, inner, mental or spiritual forms of intoxication which it becomes much more important to overcome. In the case of the person who is just beginning to be interested in the spiritual life, to avoid just the grosser forms of *moha* or mental intoxication is fair enough. But someone who is really on the path has to avoid the subtle mental intoxications as well. If you are doing this you are very unlikely to get drunk or use intoxicants such as alcohol in an unmindful way; that precept is really implicit in the other three, only raised to a higher and subtler level.

This particular formulation of ten precepts is not normally taken either by monks or by lay people in Buddhist countries in any formal, ceremonial way. There is another set of ten precepts, those taken by the *śrāmaṇera*, which are quite different from these.[14] The Ten Precepts taken by members of the Western Buddhist Order (WBO) are however traditional, indeed canonical, in origin. They are found as a list of ten skilful actions or *kusala dhammas* in the scriptures, and people are referred to as repeating and practising them, but in modern Buddhist practice (outside the WBO) they are not administered or taken ceremonially. From that point of view, although they are rooted in tradition, their formal use and practice within the WBO represents a new departure.[15]

9

Confession of Faults

The evil which I have heaped up
Through my ignorance and foolishness –
Evil in the world of everyday experience
As well as evil in understanding and intelligence –
All that I acknowledge to the Protectors.

Standing before them
With hands raised in reverence,
And terrified of suffering,
I pay salutations again and again.

May the Leaders receive this kindly,
Just as it is, with its many faults!
What is not good, O Protectors,
I shall not do again.
(Bennett)

Whatever the evil that has been accumulated by my foolishness and
ignorance, and whatever of my speaking and teaching is
objectionable, and whatever is evil by nature: I confess it all,
standing in the presence of the Lords, fearing sorrow, and with

folded hands prostrating myself again and again. May the Leaders
accept my sin and transgression! That which was not good, Lords,
will not be done again by me.
(Matics)

Essentially the confession of faults, or *pāpa deśanā*, is a recognition
of the darker side of ourselves. It is not a question of breast-beating and
bewailing our sins, but rather of a realistic appraisal of our shortcomings
and weaknesses so that they may be overcome. It also entails a resolution
that we *will* overcome that darker side of ourselves.

In order to understand more fully what the *pāpa deśanā* represents in
the context of the Sevenfold Puja, we have to recall the sequence of
devotional states represented by the three previous sections. In the
Worship section we just take delight in the beauty of the spiritual ideal.
In the Salutation we bow down before that ideal, thereby recognizing the
great distance that separates us, as we are at present, from it. When we
come to the Going for Refuge, we take courage and determine to close
the gap. We *go* for Refuge. We start actively progressing in the direction
of the spiritual goal. But once we have started making that effort we soon
find that there are all sorts of things holding us back – all sorts of bad
habits that we have formed and all kinds of unskilful actions that we have
committed. We discover that we are in a bad way in certain respects. So
the next stage is to acknowledge that, to confess it – not only in the depths
of our own hearts but also in front of the spiritual community. We thus
begin to shed some of the baggage that is hindering us from climbing
towards the mountain peak of Enlightenment. This is confession in the
Buddhist sense, and it follows on naturally from Going for Refuge.

Of course people with a Christian, especially a Catholic, background
may have quite a different idea of confession. It conjures up images of
people creeping into a little box and whispering through a grille to
someone on the other side who listens to all the sordid details and then
absolves them so they can go away all clean and pure to do it all over
again. In this case the person confessing is terrified not of suffering, the
natural consequence of evil, but of punishment, inflicted by an external
authority. These connotations of the word 'confession' have nothing to
do with the Buddhist practice of *pāpa deśanā*.

'The evil which I have heaped up' arises from the unskilful states of
mind which hold us back from Going for Refuge. At root these are all
based in greed, hatred, and delusion, even though sometimes they can
take very subtle forms. Mrs Bennett's translation, 'heaped up', works best
here. Matics's 'accumulated' evil suggests something passive like

dividends accumulating in the bank without our having to do anything about it. But 'heaped up' evil emphasizes the active part we play, heaping up evil almost like earth or sand. It even seems to emphasize the utter ridiculousness of what we are doing much of the time. We may think that we are doing all sorts of different things, but actually much of it amounts simply to heaping up evil, strengthening the bonds which hold us back on the spiritual path. This is how we pass much of our time, busily heaping up evil.

The next phrase, 'through my ignorance and foolishness', suggests the basic causes of all this unwholesome activity: ignorance in relation to fundamental principles and foolishness in relation to their application in everyday life. When we get our basic principles wrong, when we are unaware of those principles, that is ignorance. And if, despite having some awareness of the principles, we do not manage to apply them properly in everyday life, that is foolishness. Ignorance is more theoretical, foolishness more practical.

Matics's translation follows Śāntideva quite strictly in focusing on the evil actions arising out of the 'everyday experience' of a monk – i.e. out of 'speaking and teaching'. Mrs Bennett avoids this apparently narrow application of the verse, and this makes her translation more helpful.

All that I acknowledge to the Protectors.

The operative word here is 'all'. It is not easy to confess everything. Usually we fudge, we rationalize, we hold back. And we do this out of fear: fear of change; fear that we will have to give up the activity which is confessed. Very often we are willing to confess only those things that we do not care about very much, or do not really think are sins or offences. We may even confess things of which we are secretly rather proud. Confession then becomes almost a form of boasting. But the things of which we are truly ashamed, the things which we really do think are wrong or evil, we find very difficult to confess. We hardly dare even to think about them. We should always be aware of this tendency and try to see what we are holding back: whether, indeed, we are truly confessing at all. There is a difference between merely telling people about something and confessing it, and sometimes it is difficult to distinguish between the two, even to ourselves.

When we really confess, we acknowledge that what we confess is evil. We feel a degree of shame on account of it, and we are also aware that those to whom we are confessing will regard it as evil. They will not brush it aside as something insignificant, something that does not matter.

Conversely, there are actions which are only conventionally considered to be wrong. We might feel quite bad about such actions and confess them in all sincerity, only to find out – with the help of our spiritual friends – that they are not in fact unskilful, but only actions conventionally regarded as wrong. We must be careful to distinguish between natural morality – the ethical behaviour suggested by the precepts – and conventional morality, which amounts to no more than what society at large thinks we ought to do.

The hallmark of confession, then, is a feeling of shame, though even 'shame' is not the ideal word for it. 'Guilt' is certainly not the right word. Guilt is the sense of having offended some greater power on which you are emotionally dependent; if you feel guilty when you confess, you are probably suffering from the Christian idea of sin which still lingers on in our society. The feeling which accompanies genuine confession is more like intense regret, especially if the misdeed has involved harm to another person. If you realize that your foolish action has harmed someone, perhaps even irreparably, you will truly wish that you had not done it. You really will see it as evil. So confession is not just a cool, objective recognition, ticking off our actions against the precepts, but something really heartfelt. It should be an emotional experience. Most of us have had that experience at some time in our lives – the realization of having done something wrong which has resulted in pain, suffering, and inconvenience for others – and have felt very sorry and regretful on that account. We can never undo what has been done, and in some cases we cannot even make it up to the person we have wronged. It is not only irreparable but irredeemable.

There are also occasions when we know we could do something – and feel that we should do it – but for some reason we don't do it. That too can be a cause of bitter regret. We could have helped, but we did not. Acts of omission as well as acts of commission have to be confessed. In a broader sense, then, this concept of confession implies responsibility. We are responsible for our actions and our failures to act, whether skilful or unskilful, good or evil. We are the heirs of our own actions, as the Buddha says.

In these verses of confession we acknowledge our evil to 'the Protectors' or Buddhas. If we really have a sense that a Buddha or Bodhisattva is present when we say these verses, then to confess in this manner will be effective and sufficient. However, most people do not have a sufficiently vivid sense of the Buddhas as actually present, so for most of us it is necessary also to confess to other people, to spiritual friends whom we trust and respect, and who are perhaps a bit more spiritually developed than we are. If all we do is go into the shrine-room and, as it were, address the Buddha, even though we might feel quite sincere about it, it will probably not be a sufficiently concrete and vivid experience to help us change our behaviour. For one thing, we are unlikely to experience the Buddha as saying anything back to us in the way that our spiritual friends will.

> Standing before them
> With hands raised in reverence
> And terrified of suffering,
> I pay salutations again and again.

Some people are very uncomfortable with the phrase 'terrified of suffering'. They are perhaps reminded of 'hellfire' sermons designed to put the fear of God into them. However, it is not the Buddhas who inflict suffering on us, but our own evil deeds operating through the law of karma. The Buddhas are not the administrators of karma. Karma functions, as it were, automatically. There is no notion of judgement, retribution, or punishment here. The Buddhas' attitude towards us will always be one of mettā and compassion. They may not approve of some of the things we have done, but they are absolutely unwavering in their compassion, so there is no need to approach them with any sort of fear or apprehension. None the less, even a Buddha cannot take away the effects of your actions. According to the Buddhist view of the universe, karma is a simple fact of life. Just as, under the laws of physics, action and reaction are equal and opposite, so under the law of karma evil actions will sooner or later bring suffering on their perpetrator. So you should indeed feel terrified when you have committed evil actions, because you are going to suffer. By reciting the verse you are not threatening yourself with suffering or trying to bully yourself into doing things which you do not want to do. You are simply reminding yourself in a down-to-earth way that unethical actions have unpleasant consequences.[16]

People who react against such a reminder perhaps do not like to admit that they have committed evil actions, or to think that they are going to suffer. In fact they *are* terrified of suffering, but would prefer not to acknowledge that this is a result of what they themselves have done. Sometimes people have said to me that they simply are not terrified of suffering. If this is really so, it can only be due to a lack of imagination on their part.

May the leaders receive this kindly,
Just as it is, with its many faults!
What is not good, O Protectors,
I shall not do again.

There is a difference in meaning between Mrs Bennett's translation and that of Matics with regard to what the leaders are asked to accept – 'my sin and transgression' (Matics) or the confession itself (Bennett). Mrs Bennett seems to reflect the Buddhist spirit better here; it is the confession which you are asking the Buddhas to accept. If your confession is effective, there should be a definite step forward. You have come across things in yourself that you have got to overcome. When you say 'What is not good I shall not do again,' it is as if you have gone beyond your unskilful actions. You are freed from them. Once you have recognized something as evil, once you have confessed it, once the members of the spiritual community have accepted that confession and perhaps given advice, and once you have really made up your mind not to do that thing again – then you should put it behind you. In a sense you should forget all about it. As a result you will feel a freedom and lightness that will lead quite naturally into the Rejoicing in Merit, which is the next section. It is much easier to rejoice in other people's merits when you can also rejoice in your own. So there is a natural transition here, via this last line of the Confession of Faults, to the Rejoicing in Merit.

10

REJOICING IN MERIT

I rejoice with delight
In the good done by all beings,
Through which they obtain rest
With the end of suffering.
May those who have suffered be happy!

I rejoice in the release of beings
From the sufferings of the rounds of existence;
I rejoice in the nature of the Bodhisattva
And the Buddha,
Who are Protectors.

I rejoice in the arising of the Will to Enlightenment,
And the Teaching:
Those Oceans which bring happiness to all beings,
And are the abode of welfare of all beings.
(Bennett)

I rejoice in exultation at the goodness, and at the cessation and
destruction of sorrow, wrought by all beings. May those who sorrow
achieve joy! I rejoice at the release of embodied beings from the

sorrowful wheel of rebirth. I rejoice at the Bodhisattvahood and at
the Buddhahood of those who have attained salvation. I rejoice at
the Oceans of Determination, the Bearers of Happiness to all beings,
the Vehicles of Advantage for all beings, and those who teach.
(Matics)

THE TWO TRANSLATIONS SOUND QUITE DIFFERENT, especially the third
verse. Sanskrit is a difficult language with very complex grammar;
clauses can be arranged and interpreted in many different ways, especially in a piece of Sanskrit poetry. Mrs Bennett's rendering seems clearer
and more straightforward, but both are probably justified.

During the *puṇyānumodanā*, the rejoicing in merit – or virtue as it might
also be translated – we recollect the noble lives of others. We think of the
Buddhas and Bodhisattvas and great spiritual teachers – people like
Milarepa, Hui Neng, and Hakuin. We bring to mind renowned helpers
of humanity and even ordinary people whom we know personally to
have acted in noble, generous, and kindly ways. The example of all these
people provides us with enthusiasm and inspiration. Like us they are
human, and reflecting on this fact encourages us to believe that we can
become as worthy and noble as they have shown themselves to be. We
feel happy on account of their attainments and draw strength from
recollecting them.

The practice of rejoicing in merit counteracts unskilful mental states
such as jealousy, envy, pride, and egotism. It is part of the definition of a
skilful action that there should be no interest in deriving personal recognition from it. You rejoice in good deeds, but you are just as glad if
somebody else has done them as if you had done them yourself. You
don't feel inferior because somebody else has shown such good qualities,
or imagine that that person may look down on you. This kind of over-
sensitivity and over-preoccupation with oneself is unfortunately quite
common and prevents people from appreciating the good in others. We
should, then, rejoice in merits quite impersonally, just as we feel happy
that the sun is shining. We don't feel jealous that the sun sheds light when
we do not. We just rejoice that there is sunshine around making the world
a brighter and better place.

In the context of the Sevenfold Puja, Rejoicing in Merits represents the
converse of the Confession of Faults. You have freed yourself from faults,
so you feel happy and delighted; and being happy and delighted with
yourself, you can feel happy and delighted with others. This is an
important psychological fact: you cannot be happy with others unless
you are first of all happy with yourself. Rejoicing in merit requires a basis

of mettā and you cannot really feel mettā for others unless you feel mettā for yourself. Your feelings about yourself and your feelings about others are very intimately connected. It is noticeable, for instance, that people who are feeling guilty because they are out of touch with their own spiritual practice find it very difficult to appreciate what others are doing. They even sometimes adopt a resentful or highly critical attitude towards other people's efforts, and find it quite impossible to rejoice in their merits. By contrast, if you see someone genuinely, freely, and regularly rejoicing in the merits of others, you can be sure that that person is very much at peace with him or herself.

You may of course be doing what you ought to be doing and still not feel any sense of joy. In this case you may be doing the right things in an external sense only, going through the motions without the appropriate mental and emotional attitude. You are just 'being good' – and that can make you all the more resentful because you think 'Here I am being good, but I don't seem to be getting any results from it. I'm not even *feeling* good.' But sometimes, going through the motions, if you do it consciously and mindfully, helps you to develop the corresponding mental and emotional attitude, and probably an element of that 'disciplinary' approach is necessary for most people. We can't always have skilful mental states before we do skilful actions. Sometimes our unskilful mental states are so powerful that we just have to perform skilful actions anyway, and then gradually try to bring our mental states into line with our actions.

It is an aspect both of ritual and of ethical observance to perform actions which will only subsequently enable you to develop appropriate mental states. Of course, if you adopt this approach, you must understand what you are doing and why – otherwise you can end up losing touch with what you are doing and feeling. A person who is naturally in touch with his or her own feelings should be able to do this quite safely, but a person with a tendency to 'be good' without experiencing his or her true feelings should have recourse to this approach only with extreme caution.

But although we should observe caution in acting at variance with our feelings, it is not, as some would suggest, hypocritical to do so. If you feel like murdering somebody but you don't actually do it you are not thereby being a hypocrite. You would only be a hypocrite if, when asked about your feelings towards that person, you said 'Oh, I absolutely love him.' Hypocrisy is consciously and deliberately trying to give an impression that your mental state or behaviour is other than it really is, for purely selfish reasons.

Within the spiritual community you should be able to own up to all your unskilful thoughts and feelings. It is also very important when you are practising the Mettā Bhāvanā, the cultivation of loving kindness, to keep in touch with how you really feel rather than feigning feelings of mettā because that is what you 'should' be feeling. Even if what you feel is crude and negative, as long as you are experiencing it consciously, you can begin to work on it and gradually refine it, sublimate it, and make it more positive. But if you are out of touch with how you feel to begin with, what can you possibly do?

The factors in society which lead to people's emotions becoming repressed are quite complex. But whatever the causes may be, when this happens people become unable to rejoice in the merits of others. Clearly it is something that goes very deep. Without strongly developed positive emotions you can't have much individual development. And being emotionally positive has two aspects: feeling happy with yourself and feeling happy with others, or in other words rejoicing in their merits.

I rejoice with delight
In the good done by all beings,
Through which they obtain rest
With the end of suffering.
May those who have suffered be happy!

I rejoice in the release of beings
From the sufferings of the rounds of existence.

We rejoice in the merits of all those who have gained Enlightenment. Even though this is a Mahāyāna work, these lines express very much the standpoint of the Hīnayāna 'doctrine follower' (as opposed to the 'faith-follower') until we come to:

I rejoice in the nature of the Bodhisattva
And the Buddha,
Who are Protectors.

You rejoice in their nature. It is as though you are saying 'Even apart from their functions – teaching, helping, and guiding me – I rejoice in their very nature as Enlightened Ones.' It is intrinsically delightful and you rejoice in it quite disinterestedly. This is like the Worship section raised to a much higher level, because your understanding has deepened.

I rejoice in the arising of the Will to Enlightenment,
And the Teaching:

Those Oceans which bring happiness to all beings,
And are the abode of welfare of all beings.

You rejoice in the arising of the Will to Enlightenment wherever it occurs – both in yourself and in others. The bodhicitta and the Dharma are 'Oceans' in the sense that they are unlimited just as the ocean is unlimited – poetically speaking, if not literally. These verses convey the attitude of rejoicing in whatever is good in the past, present, and future; rejoicing in the good deeds that people do, their skilful actions, their observance of the precepts, their Going for Refuge, and their practice of the pāramitās; and also rejoicing in the transcendental nature of the Buddhas and Bodhisattvas and the Will to Enlightenment.

If you have this attitude of rejoicing, you are in a very positive mental and emotional state. Your delight in people's good deeds can be seen as a delight in the reflection of the Buddha nature in other people. If you rejoice in the Buddha, you cannot but rejoice in the meritorious actions even of an unenlightened being, because those good deeds reflect or anticipate, however faintly and distantly, Enlightenment itself. Conversely, if as a Buddhist you fail to rejoice in the merits of those who are clearly progressing on the spiritual path, you are practising a form of dishonesty, keeping silent about what in your heart you know to be worthy of recognition. It's a sort of passive lie.

We should rejoice in the merits not just of individuals but of the spiritual community as a whole. We don't always realize just how precarious the whole structure of the spiritual community is in our world. In the first place, society itself is somewhat precarious. Then superimposed on society is a structure of civilization and culture which is even more precarious. And superimposed on that is a spiritual community which is very precarious indeed. It would be quite easy for someone in power who wanted to do so to wipe out the entire Western Buddhist Order, at least within a particular country. In some states this could be done without anyone knowing or noticing that those few hundred people had been rounded up and eliminated. It is not very difficult to dispose of, say, a hundred people, eliminating a spiritual community in a particular region at a stroke. It is not even all that difficult to wipe out an entire civilization and culture. Think of the libraries that have been burned down, the monuments that have been destroyed, the scholars who have been killed, the religions that have been wiped out. Look, for instance, at the destruction of Buddhism in India by Islam; or, in our own day, what has happened to Buddhist culture in parts of south-east Asia, in China, and in Tibet. The destruction of cultures is bad enough, but in some areas like Tibet, a spiritual community has almost been wiped out, with what remains having been driven either underground or beyond the borders.

The events of the twentieth century have shattered Western political optimism for most thinking people. The last world war and especially the extermination of the Jews shocked anybody who could think seriously because it showed the fragility of civilization and culture. The Germans were one of the most civilized and cultured peoples in Europe – maybe not *en masse*, but they have produced the greatest philosophers and musicians as well as many great scientists and statesmen. They have made a major contribution to Western culture for centuries, yet virtually the whole German population apparently connived at the murder, as one can only call it, of perhaps six million people. What a sobering reminder of the barbarism that underlies civilization and culture! And it could happen in other countries too. We may like to think it could not happen in dear old Britain, but under certain circumstances perhaps it could. This realization has destroyed the idea that things can be permanently changed and improved almost by Act of Parliament. We can no longer think – if we ever did – that we have only to change social institutions and we will have heaven on earth.

All this is not so surprising if we take a longer-term view. After all, civilization as we know it is only ten or twelve thousand years old, and the great religions have had only two to two-and-a-half thousand years to influence us – even assuming that all of them were positive to begin with. But humanity has been around for three hundred and fifty thousand years in the form of *homo sapiens*, and two million years if we go back to *homo erectus* and *homo habilis*. Humanity was not completely uncivilized during all that period because it developed tribal organization which represents a degree of culture, but we can look even further back to our semi-human ancestry, which existed over four million years ago. Many scientists believe that we are descended from carnivorous apes (the smaller variety of *australopithecus*). So we must not be too complacent. We must not think that the upward movement is an easy task. Civilization can break down; it can decline and fall. The Buddhist view is that civilization and culture go through cycles. We climb up to higher civilization, then we sink down to barbarism, and this cycle repeats itself. Progress is not necessarily going to carry on indefinitely. There is only one context – an individual context – in which progress is assured, and that is the transcendental part of the spiral path – beyond Stream-entry. All mundane things are governed by cyclical movement, human society included.

An Enlightened humanity or Enlightened society is therefore an impossibility, a contradiction in terms, even though Enlightened individuals may be emerging all the time. This is because the factors that are required to keep humanity – in the ordinary sense – going are the opposite of the factors that constitute Enlightenment. If one were able somehow to organize society so that it was conducive to spiritual development, would one even, to take a very ordinary example, choose to propagate the race? If one could somehow halt the growth of the population and only encourage the existing individuals until they gradually all became Enlightened – one would have to arrange for them to live for a very long time too – we would end up with an Enlightened society. But new beings are constantly being born. In a karmic sense, we don't even know where they have come from. For all we know, they may have come straight out of some hell realm – and you are unlikely to come out of that in a very positive frame of mind.

We will always have 'little devils' being born into the world as well as 'little angels', and even one devil can spoil it for all the angels just by being a nuisance. If one person shouts during the meditation, that spoils it for everybody else. One country that wants to fight can upset the peace of the whole world. If you like you can work to improve things, but the danger of putting all your energy into improving the world outside instead of balancing that with working on yourself so that you reach a higher level of awareness is that you get dragged down by other people's negativity and destructive behaviour.

We must be quite realistic about these things. Maintaining a positive society in which the spiritual community can flourish is not easy. At the same time we must not be despondent or feel that we are living in a 'dark age' in some sense. Looking back over history, it is hard to identify any age that is clearly better than any other. In some ways ours is a very good age. Since the second world war there has not been a really big war anywhere in the world, nothing on the scale of the first two world wars. We have kept relatively peaceable over the last forty-five years, compared to previous ages. There is the terrible possibility of an nuclear war, but apart from that the human race has never lived, materially speaking, so comfortably or happily as at present, at least in the Western world. The standard of living has never been so high for so many people. The things that we enjoy now were enjoyed in the past only by members of aristocracies and not always even by them. Many diseases have been more or less brought under control. Yet still there can be no complete end to suffering for humanity or indeed for beings in general. There may be the end of suffering for certain individuals but so long as saṁsāra exists – and so far as we know saṁsāra always has existed and always will – suffering is inherent in it.[17] However great the number of individuals gaining Enlightenment, the saṁsāra is beginningless and always producing, as it were, unenlightened individuals. So the Bodhisattva's work is never done.

The spiritual community will always exist within a wider community which contains both positive and negative elements. It is important, therefore, for those leading the spiritual life not to lose contact with the wider community, because that is where our energies come from. We must keep in touch with society, but we must not allow those energies to get out of control, and this is a difficult balance to preserve. The most positive sort of community in the broadest sense would be one that gave scope to all those cruder energies and forces, but was at the same time open-ended with regard to the possibility of higher development. We need a spiritual community which is uncompromising in its pursuit of the highest ideals, but which remains in contact with a wider positive group. If the spiritual community were out of touch with everyone else, where would new members come from? There is a sort of hierarchy or gradation of spiritual development and commitment, with many intermediate levels.

In practice, a Buddhist experiences life in terms of a dualism between skilful and unskilful activity, even though Buddhism teaches that ultimately such dualisms can be transcended. In practical terms, life is a constant struggle. And even when the struggle is over for us individually, if we look at society we find there is still a lot to be done. Even if you have finished your own task, attained your own Enlightenment, you still have an infinite number of tasks to do for those around you. You will never be able to settle down and rest, nor would you want to. If you are a Bodhisattva, it is your nature to help beings. You are inherently compassionate. Light cannot help being light any more than darkness can help being darkness. When we rejoice in merits, we are rejoicing in this light, in this principle of Bodhisattvahood at work in the world. We are recalling just how greatly precious it is, especially when we reflect on what life would be like without it.

11

ENTREATY AND SUPPLICATION

Saluting them with folded hands
I entreat the Buddhas in all the quarters:
May they make shine the lamp of the Dharma
For those wandering in the suffering of delusion!

With hands folded in reverence
I implore the Conquerors desiring to enter Nirvāṇa:
May they remain here for endless ages,
So that life in this world does not grow dark.
(Bennett)

With folded hands, I beseech the perfect Buddhas in all places: may they cause the light of the Dharma to shine upon those who, because of confusion, have fallen into sorrow. With folded hands, I beseech the Conquerors who are desirous of experiencing cessation: may they pause for countless aeons, lest this world become blind.
(Matics)

THERE IS NO SIGNIFICANT DIFFERENCE between these two translations. What essentially is happening in the sixth section, the *adhyeṣaṇā* and *yācanā*, entreaty and supplication, is that we are developing receptivity, expressing our readiness to be taught. Very often people, even religious people, are not really ready to be taught – so we have to make ourselves ready. We have after all been rejoicing in the good qualities of the Buddhas and Bodhisattvas, as well as the arising of the Will to Enlightenment and the Teaching. Now we make ourselves receptive to all those things, and especially of course to the Buddha and the Dharma. But before we go further into the subject of receptivity, let us have a look at the components of this section of the Sevenfold Puja.

The first verse recalls a particular episode from the scriptures, the famous request of Brahmā Sahampati, the 'lord of a thousand worlds'. Shortly after the Buddha's Enlightenment Brahmā Sahampati appeared before him and pleaded with him to teach others the way to gain Enlightenment. Through this appeal he overcame the Buddha's initial inclination to think that the Dharma was just too difficult and subtle to be communicated. So here we adopt the attitude of respectful entreaty of Brahmā Sahampati. We ask the Buddha to teach. This does not mean that the Buddhas do not teach unless they are asked to; they are always ready. But they cannot teach us unless we are open to their teaching. In this section we express our openness. Indeed, the expression is in a way part of the openness. If we really want something, we ask for it; the asking is a natural extension of the wanting.

Suppose you want something from someone but you are somehow reluctant to make this clear to them. Perhaps you want to borrow some money from a friend; you just need a couple of pounds quickly. You know that they have it and that they would be quite willing to lend it to you, but somehow you hesitate to ask, to make your need known. This sort of situation suggests reserve, holding back, lack of confidence. It may arise from feelings of guilt, or it may be that you are reluctant to put yourself in the position of possibly being refused. This is analogous to a reluctance sometimes to ask for spiritual teaching. Perhaps you feel you are not worthy of it – or perhaps you fear that you might get more than you bargained for. You might indeed *get* some spiritual teaching, not just a little pat on the head. This is especially the case with approaching Zen masters. If you ask them for a teaching you really take your life in your hands. People say they want to be taught, but it is not all that easy to find those who really do want to learn in a truly spiritual sense. So it is good to express your willingness and readiness to learn, to make it absolutely clear that you are open, that you want to be receptive. Incidentally, the same principle applies to asking for ordination. Sometimes people adopt the attitude 'I won't actually ask because when I am ready, people will know and they will just tell me.' This also suggests a certain lack of openness which needs to be overcome.

In the first verse you 'entreat the Buddhas in all the quarters' – not just the Buddhas in your own immediate environment. You are thinking of others as well as yourself. You are requesting not only that you yourself may have teaching, but also that the 'lamp of the Dharma' should be made to shine on all living beings. You want to keep the channels of communication open between the mundane and the transcendental for all beings, for the whole world.

I remember a friend once strongly objecting to the line: 'For those wandering in the suffering of delusion'. He said that he did not feel that he *was* wandering in the suffering of delusion. But of course those who are deluded may not be aware that they are deluded. And while you might not be suffering at present, if you are deluded, the suffering will come sooner or later.

In the second verse we:

… implore the Conquerors desiring to enter Nirvāṇa:
May they remain here for endless ages,
So that life in this world does not grow dark.

This too is based on an episode from the Buddha's life in the scriptures. How genuine it is we do not know, but in the *Mahā-parinibbāna Sutta*[18] the Buddha gives Ānanda a broad hint that, if he was asked, he would stay on in the world until the end of the kalpa. Commentators differ in their interpretation of this. Some say that 'kalpa' here means the full term of natural life, i.e. a hundred years; others say it means until the end of the world period. In any case, Ānanda failed to take the hint, due to the intervention of Māra, and the Buddha therefore passed away. It is rather an odd episode and there is no general agreement on what it really means, even supposing it did actually happen. Did the Buddha need to be asked to stay on for the remainder of his hundred years, or until the end of the aeon? Is it a warning that we, like Ānanda in this incident, are ceasing to be receptive? I believe we may take it to mean that there is no end to the need for entreaty. You must not think that once you have asked a Bodhisattva to stay and teach, that is that. You have to go on asking and wanting and being receptive. In other words, don't take a Buddha or Bodhisattva for granted – even when he has been preaching for forty-five years. Be aware that he might disappear at any minute, because saṁsāra is so painful and the pull of nirvāṇa, which is within his reach, is so strong. Unless you constantly keep your need before him and are really open to him, he might just disappear into nirvāṇa. So don't let your attention waver for an instant.

However, there is another way of looking at this incident. It shows that spiritual teaching depends upon you. If you are not listening to the Buddhas and Bodhisattvas, how can they be said to teach? And if they are not teaching, they might as well be in nirvāṇa. Indeed you put them into nirvāṇa, you make them inoperative. How could it be otherwise? The minute your attention slackens or you turn away, they are unable to teach because there is no one there to teach, no resonance. Teaching does not mean emitting words; it means communicating with beings who are listening. The Teachers can break through your inattentiveness, but if you really don't want to be receptive, there is nothing even they can do about it. If you want, you can silence all the Buddhas and Bodhisattvas. It is a terrible thought. You can put out the lamp, certainly for yourself, perhaps even for others. To change the metaphor, you've banged the door in the Buddha's face, so what can he do? He must just sit quietly on the other side until you open it again. You might even forget there was a door there at all, and then you wouldn't be able to tell other people who might not know about it, until finally no one would know that there was a door there to be opened, and it would remain shut for a very long time. So you must keep up your entreaty to keep the Buddhas teaching.

In other words, there is no absolute distinction between a Buddha's activity, if I may call it that, and other beings' receptivity. They go together. If you are receptive, he will be active. If he is active, it means you have at least started to be receptive. You could say that if other beings do not allow him to teach, it is as though the Buddha's own Enlightenment, even, is not complete. This is putting it rather strongly but it gives us something to think about. Perhaps there is no such thing as absolute self-sufficiency, even for a Buddha. It is not easy to describe what the Buddha's experience is like in terms of unenlightened experience, so let us take an ordinary human analogy. Suppose you like somebody in a normal, healthy way. If they are aware of that and like you back, doesn't that give an extra dimension to the fact of your liking them? Or is your liking exactly the same whether they like you or not? Or take the case of ordinary teaching. Without the stimulus of the students' curiosity and interest and alertness and receptivity, no teaching can take place.

This notion of interdependence is expressed in another way in the Bodhisattva ideal, in accordance with which the Bodhisattva vows not to enter nirvāṇa until all beings have crossed over the ocean of suffering. If people really want to stay in that ocean of suffering, it follows that they are holding the Bodhisattva back. In a sense his Enlightenment is not complete until they too become Enlightened. So it's as though the Buddha is begging sentient beings to let him teach.

It is significant that the Entreaty and Supplication comes after the Rejoicing in Merits, which is a very bright, almost radiant state in which you are intensely aware of the merits of other beings, especially the merits of the Buddhas and Bodhisattvas. Out of this awareness you rejoice, and in that rejoicing, positive state you become receptive. You open yourself to the influence of the Buddhas and Bodhisattvas, to the Dharma itself, as it were, there being no Dharma apart from the Buddhas or Bodhisattvas who communicate it.

Very often, however, we are not positive enough to be receptive in this way. We may be afraid of the change that receptivity might initiate, unable to cope, almost. Or we may think we know it all already. There is a little story about a Zen master which concerns this sort of attitude. According to this tale, a university professor went to call on a Zen master to ask the master to teach him. The Zen master received him very politely and, as is the custom, offered him tea. The master then placed two cups on a low table and started pouring tea from the pot into one of the cups. He continued pouring until the cup was full and then went on pouring. The professor watched the tea overflow into the saucer, but the Zen master just went on pouring. Soon the saucer was full to overflowing, so that tea streamed across the tablecloth, and still the Zen master went on pouring. By the time a little rivulet was flowing right on to the floor, the professor could contain himself no longer. He knew that Zen masters were reputed to be pretty queer, but this one was the most eccentric he had ever come across. 'Why are you still pouring?' he asked. 'The cup is full.' The Zen master now looked up from his pouring. 'Why do you come here?' he replied. 'Your cup is full.' And he continued: 'Unless you empty your cup, you cannot receive anything. No use expecting me to pour into a full cup.' So we have to make ourselves empty in order to receive – not literally, because we cannot forget everything we know, but we can put it to one side, as it were, so that it will not get in the way.

Even if you are initially receptive to spiritual experience, it can still be difficult to cope with the consequences of that experience. When you 'open up' and receive spiritual teaching or spiritual experience, the initial experience needs to be followed up by a process of assimilation. This is analogous to the path of vision being followed by the path of transformation. But in order to assimilate the experience, to transform your being in accordance with that experience, you may need to spend time in suitably supportive conditions. Otherwise you can be like the snake in the Indian saying who is trying to swallow a frog which is too big. It is so big he can't get it down but because of the way his fangs curve, he cannot vomit it up either. Through being genuinely open it can sometimes happen that you go through a period of 'spiritual indigestion' when you can be quite unbalanced. There are stories about Zen masters – that is, stories about them before they became Zen masters – where they appear to other people to be quite mad.

It would be wrong to say that you could have too much receptivity, any more than you could have too much awareness or too much mindfulness. However, it may be that sometimes when you have been receptive you are unable, for the time being at least, to handle that experience. You are, as it were, midway between the path of vision and the path of transformation, and that can be quite an uncomfortable state. For this reason spiritual teachers should be aware of the possibility of pushing people too hard or too far, of opening them up too much during retreats and similar activities – especially if the next day they go back to the everyday world, back to their jobs and families. People need time to make some headway on the path of transformation corresponding to whatever level of the path of vision they have experienced.

When we perform the Sevenfold Puja, immediately after the verses of Entreaty and Supplication we usually have a reading from the scriptures, as is appropriate after opening ourselves to the teaching. In fact, the verses of the puja suggest the attitude with which we should always hear or read the Buddha's words. Immediately after the reading we recite the *Heart Sūtra*, which contains the essence of the teaching, at least from a Mahāyāna point of view.[19] There may also be readings at other stages of the puja, according to the nature of the occasion.

If you happen to be asked to do a reading – and it is to be hoped that the leader of the puja will give you plenty of notice of this – you should read through it a few times beforehand to be sure you fully understand the structure of the sentences and where the emphases should come. Readings from the scriptures will be in translation, which often means that the structures of sentences are quite awkward and complex, so you need to get the hang of them. If possible it might even be best to read the passage aloud beforehand, preferably with someone listening to offer comments and suggestions. Not many people are able to read well without making this sort of effort.

Tone of voice and enunciation are very important too. A reading should not be delivered in a harsh or discordant tone. It does, however, need to be clear. Oral communication, in readings and in a great many other contexts, is a vital practical element of the spiritual life. For those who are not very skilled at it, it is well worth while making the effort to improve, enlisting the help of friends and even undertaking formal training if necessary.

If you are listening to the reading, it is obviously important to remain attentive and receptive throughout. During the reading you are less active than during the verses of the puja itself since you are not reciting or chanting anything, so there may be a temptation to use it as an opportunity to stretch your legs and mentally withdraw somewhat from the puja. But it would be a great pity if, having just declared your openness to the Buddha's teaching, you then failed to receive it.

12

Transference of Merit and Self-surrender

May the merit gained
In my acting thus
Go to the alleviation of the suffering of all beings.
My personality throughout my existences,
My possessions,
And my merit in all three ways,
I give up without regard to myself
For the benefit of all beings.

Just as the earth and other elements
Are serviceable in many ways
To the infinite number of beings
Inhabiting limitless space;
So may I become
That which maintains all beings
Situated throughout space,
So long as all have not attained
To peace.
(Bennett)

Having done all this, let me also be a cause of abatement, by means of whatever good I have achieved, for all of the sorrow of all creatures.... I sacrifice indifferently my bodies, pleasures, and goodness, where the three ways cross, past, present and future, for the complete fulfilment of the welfare of all beings.... As the earth and other elements are, in various ways, for the enjoyment of innumerable beings dwelling in all of space; so may I be, in various ways, the means of sustenance for the living beings occupying space, for as long a time as all are not satisfied.
(Matics)

THERE IS ONE DIFFERENCE IN INTERPRETATION in the second verse. Matics specifies 'past, present, and future' whereas Mrs Bennett's 'merit in all three ways' refers to another traditional formulation: merit by way of body, speech, and mind. Whichever of these interpretations we follow, the general meaning is clear. You give up *all* your merit – past, present, and future, through body, speech, and mind. You don't want any of it just for yourself. According to some traditional texts there are three possible aims in life. You can wish for well-being in this present life; you can hope for a good and happy rebirth in some future existence; or you can think in terms of gaining Enlightenment for the benefit of all beings. In reciting these verses, it is the third kind of motivation you are trying to cultivate.

Thus the overall feeling of this section is one of altruism and service to other beings, 'just as the earth and other elements are serviceable in many ways'. There are many references in Buddhist tradition to the idea that the elements are for everybody. Everybody can stand on the earth and make use of the earth; everybody breathes the air; everybody drinks and makes use of water. They are free to all; they belong to all; they are completely at the service of all living beings. And the Bodhisattva aspires to be like that – to be available to all living beings, of service to them, enjoyed by them, without any restriction or limitation. And just as everybody equally breathes air, in the same way the Bodhisattva wants to be equally of service to all.

The phrase 'that which maintains all beings' refers to *ākāśa*, which is translated sometimes as 'space', sometimes as 'ether'. It is the subtle element (as opposed to the gross elements of earth, water, fire, and air) that sustains the gross elements as they sustain living beings, and under-lies the entire physical universe. So the Bodhisattva aspires not only to be like earth, fire, water, and air but to be like *ākāśa*, which contains and supports the elements themselves. Beyond even that is the idea of Dharma, in the sense here of cosmic law – the word *Dharma* coming from the verb meaning 'to support'. Ultimately you could say that it is the Dharma that supports everything.

In these verses of Transference of Merit and Self-surrender, you give up not only all your possessions but even your merit. You do not want even to keep your own goodness – your own means, as it were, of getting to nirvāṇa – for yourself. This is certainly one of the most difficult things to do – to give up your own merits, give up, in a way, your own reputation.

Hakuin, the famous Zen master, is a great example in this respect. According to one story, he was once wrongly accused of making a young woman in the village pregnant, and he thereby lost his reputation as a venerable Zen monk and Zen master. When the child was born, the young woman just put it on the temple doorstep, so Hakuin took it in and brought it up. After some years the woman repented and confessed that she had falsely accused him of being the father of the child in order to shield someone else, so he gave the child back. But in all those years he never said anything about the situation except 'Is it so?' When people said 'This girl is accusing you of being the father of her child,' he simply said 'Is it so?' When they said it was his child and he had better bring it up, his response was the same. And when the woman admitted that her accusation had been false and reclaimed the child, again he just said 'Is it so?' At no point was he concerned about his own reputation as a virtuous Zen master.

Hakuin, then, had no attachment to his own merit, unlike many people who are very attached to their reputations. From an ordinary human point of view such concern for one's own good name is understandable, but from the highest spiritual point of view it is our attachment which must be given up. The Bodhisattva doesn't mind appearing not to be a Bodhisattva or even not to be a good person, if that is necessary. He certainly doesn't want to keep his merit to himself so that he can get to nirvāṇa ahead of other beings. If a sense of ego is the principal obstacle standing between you and Enlightenment, how could you ever get to Enlightenment with your ego simply accumulating good actions which it regarded as its own? Clearly that kind of outlook cannot take you all the way.

In this final section of the Sevenfold Puja you say, as it were: 'I know I have performed this puja; I have saluted the Buddhas and Bodhisattvas, gone for Refuge, confessed my faults and rejoiced in merits. I have entreated the Buddhas and Bodhisattvas to preach and opened myself to their influence. But I do not claim anything of that merit just for myself. May it redound to the spiritual benefit of all living beings, because that is all I am really interested in.' It is called Transference of Merit and Self-surrender because here you have virtually surrendered yourself. You don't have any selfish interest even in your own good actions. You don't wish to claim them or appropriate them just for yourself. From a Mahā-yāna point of view, no virtuous action is really complete until the merit from it has been dedicated to all beings. This practice transforms what would otherwise be a means to a purely individual attainment into something much bigger, much more universal. We should therefore have this attitude of dedicating or transferring the merit gained by any positive activity we undertake, and especially by ritual acts like the puja.

The doctrine of *pariṇāmanā* or transference of merit is not meant to assert that anything has literally been transferred from one person to another. It is to be understood in a more poetic sense; it concerns our inner attitude. For instance, in Burmese temples, whenever anyone makes an offering they ring the bell – the idea being that you wish that whoever hears the bell may share in the merits of the offering that has just been made. The doctrine arises because, owing to the very structure and nature of language, we cannot help speaking about the spiritual life to some extent in terms of accumulation – gaining this, developing that, attaining the other. If we are not careful, this can lead us into a kind of refined selfishness. To counteract that tendency, and to prevent us from thinking of our merits as literally our own, as attaching to our egos, we have this doctrine. It says 'Yes, develop virtues, acquire all the wonderful Bodhi-sattva qualities, but share them.' The same sort of idea exists, in a simple form, even in Hīnayāna Buddhism.

We cannot of course sincerely wish to transfer our merits unless we feel very positively towards other beings. The Transference of Merit and Self-surrender is therefore a form, or an extension, of the Mettā Bhāvanā practice. It is a training in egolessness and paves the way for the arising of the bodhicitta. Indeed the whole Sevenfold Puja is oriented towards encouraging the arising of the bodhicitta, towards creating the conditions in which it can arise.

What exactly is meant, then, by the bodhicitta? 'Bodhicitta' literally means 'the thought of or will to Enlightenment', but the main point to grasp is that it is not someone's individual will in the narrow sense. You do, of course, have to start off with an individual will making an individual effort, but the bodhicitta is something which as it were supervenes upon that individual spiritual effort when it reaches a very high degree of purity, refinement, positivity, and openness. It is as if the stream or tendency making for Enlightenment takes you over. That is where the surrender comes in. You surrender yourself to it, open yourself to it, become a channel for it. You are no longer 'you' in a narrow egoistic sense. There is something higher working through you. You are still recognizably there as an individual living being functioning in the world, but in fact it is not just you functioning – it is the bodhicitta functioning, moving in the direction of the Enlightenment of all beings.

This is why I have sometimes said that the bodhicitta manifests within the context of the spiritual community. It is not individual, but it is not collective either; it is in a third category, like the spiritual community itself. The spiritual community, especially to the extent that it is a transcendental community, is an embodiment of the bodhicitta. Just as on the ordinary level you can have a wave of emotion that sweeps through a crowd, which is sub-individual, in the same way you can have the bodhicitta manifesting in the midst of the spiritual community, which is supra-individual. When that happens you feel that you are working for something greater than yourself, although there is really no distinction between you and it. Even though a number of individuals are involved, it is not a mass thing, precisely because they are individuals. In a sense you cannot have just one lone Bodhisattva, although it may seem that you can. By thinking of the bodhicitta as arising within the spiritual community, you safeguard yourself against thinking of it as an individual phenomenon. You could say that the bodhicitta is something that manifests when a number of individuals in a spiritual community have reached the point represented by the last stage of the Sevenfold Puja. If you have performed your Sevenfold Puja with real feeling, as you reach the end of it there should be an experience somewhat like the arising of the bodhicitta.

There is some similarity between this and the Hīnayāna concept of Stream-entry, although it is always very difficult to correlate Hīnayāna doctrinal formulations which have become rather rigid with Mahāyāna doctrinal formulations which have perhaps become equally rigid. Loosening both concepts up and trying to get at what they were originally referring to, I would say that in the full sense the arising of the bodhicitta is something that happens after Stream-entry. You can certainly have an aspiration towards Buddhahood and a very sincere dedication to the Bodhisattva way of life long before you become a Stream-entrant, but the arising of the bodhicitta as a total experience only takes place, I believe, after Stream-entry. This said, within the context of the spiritual community, individuals who are not Stream-entrants can still get some taste of the bodhicitta, so to speak, even though it will not be a full arising. They may not be 'flowers' themselves but they can at least enjoy the fragrance of those who are flowers.

Furthermore, they can act in the Bodhisattva spirit to whatever extent they are capable of doing so. Just as the Bodhisattva aspires to give whatever support he can to the beings of the whole cosmos, so on your own level, if you are at least trying to practise the Bodhisattva ideal, that should naturally involve giving whatever support you can to those within your immediate environment, your spiritual community. If you are not functioning in a supportive way, if you just regard the spiritual community as a sort of convenience to your individual development, you are living more in accordance with the Arhant ideal, indeed the narrowest interpretation of the Arhant ideal. Taken in this narrow, extreme form, that ideal becomes self-defeating, because you cannot really help yourself without helping others. If you think in terms of helping yourself to the exclusion of helping others, you have a very rigid idea of self and of others, and as long as that fixed view is there you can't even gain Enlightenment for yourself.

Helping ourselves involves helping others; helping others involves helping ourselves. We cannot separate the two. We cannot really use the spiritual community just as a convenience for our own individual spiritual development, even though we may try to do so. The sharing of merit which helps us move towards the Bodhisattva ideal is in accordance with the reality of our situation as living beings.

13

Concluding Mantras

THE EIGHT MANTRAS WHICH WE CHANT at the end of the puja, each one three times in call and response, are:

Oṁ maṇi padme hūṁ (Avalokiteśvara)
Oṁ a ra pa cha na dhīḥ (Mañjuśrī)
Oṁ Vajrapāṇi hūṁ (Vajrapāṇi)
Oṁ Tāre tuttāre ture svāhā (Tārā)
Oṁ Amideva hrīḥ (Amitābha)
Oṁ muni muni mahā muni Śākyamuni svāhā (Śākyamuni)
Oṁ āḥ hūṁ vajra guru Padma siddhi hūṁ (Padmasambhava)
Gate gate pāragate pārasaṁgate bodhi svāhā (Prajñapāramitā)

There are of course a great many other Buddhas and Bodhisattvas, all with their own mantras. These eight include several of the best-known and most prominent of them. But before we are introduced to them, we need to ask a fundamental question. What is a mantra?

The word *mantra* is sometimes translated as 'magic words' or even 'spell', but these renderings have quite the wrong connotations. If we turn to the etymological meaning of the word, that is a little more helpful – but not very much. Etymologically, mantra can be defined as 'that which protects the mind'. The recitation of a mantra undoubtedly does protect the mind, but so does every other spiritual practice, so this definition, whilst not actually misleading, is not nearly specific enough.

Essentially the mantra is a sound symbol – just as the figure of a Buddha or Bodhisattva is a form and colour symbol – of a particular aspect of the Enlightened mind. In referring to sound here, I do not just mean the external sound produced by the voice. Mantric sound is also internal – indeed, it is more internal than external. Sometimes the efficacy of mantras is misleadingly explained in terms of physical vibrations. It is said that the recitation of a particular mantra produces a certain number of vibrations per second which is in some way spiritually efficacious, but this is much too crude and materialistic an account. Lama Govinda has pointed out that if mantras were a matter of physical vibrations, one could simply buy a recording of them being chanted and play it over and over again to get all the wonderful spiritual benefits.

So a mantra is essentially an *inner* sound, an inner vibration, even an inner feeling. I am not suggesting that the external physical sound has no meaning at all, or that mantras should not be recited aloud; but the gross repetition of a mantra is only a means to, a catalyst for, the inner feeling of the mantra vibrating through one's being. The relationship between the gross, external, verbal repetition and the subtle, internal, mental repetition is not unlike that between a painted picture of a Buddha or Bodhisattva and that same figure visualized during meditation. In each case the gross experience leads towards the subtle experience.

But although the various translations are not much help, there are certain things one can say about a mantra, and these taken together might even add up to a definition. First, it is a string of syllables which sometimes, but not always, form or include a word or words. Whether forming words or not, the syllables of a mantra come from the sixty-four letters of the Sanskrit alphabet. It is customary not to translate mantras. It is sometimes said that they are never translated, but this is not quite correct because occasionally they are. For instance, the Padmasambhava mantra we chant as one of the concluding mantras (*oṁ āḥ hūṁ vajra guru Padma siddhi hūṁ*) differs from the one that we often chant earlier in the puja (*oṁ āḥ hūṁ jetsun guru Padma siddhi hūṁ*) inasmuch as the latter is derived from the Tibetan chanting and substitutes a Tibetan word for a Sanskrit one. The purely Sanskrit version is really the correct form, but the Tibetans do sometimes translate odd words into their own language when chanting and singing. It is not at all unusual to have different versions of mantras, if only because of mispronunciations. With the Tārā mantra, for instance, Tibetans pronounce *tāre tuttāre* as if it were *tāre tittāre*. Likewise, in the Avalokiteśvara mantra they say *oṁ maṇi peme hūṁ*.

On the other hand some Tibetans chant an alternative version of the Śākyamuni mantra: *oṁ muni muni mahāmuni Śākyamuniye svāhā*. And this is quite correct inasmuch as *ye* represents a dative inflexion – i.e. *muniye* means 'to the sage'. But this dative inflexion isn't really necessary in the context of mantras so it can safely be dropped. The one inflexion we do retain is *me* in *oṁ maṇi padme hūṁ,*.

The second thing to say about mantras is that they are not susceptible to logical analysis. In a sense, they are meaningless. Confounding any attribution of conventional meaning is what they are all about. There are certain mantras which contain words that have assignable meanings. There is, for instance, the famous mantra associated with Avalokiteśvara, *oṁ maṇi padme hūṁ*. *Maṇi* means 'jewel' and *padme* means 'in the lotus', so the middle part of the mantra could be given a literal meaning ('the jewel in the lotus'), although the initial '*oṁ*' and the concluding '*hūṁ*' could not be interpreted in any such way. But even though the phrase 'the jewel in the lotus' suggests a perfectly good philosophical meaning with all sorts of ramifications in Buddhist thought and practice, it would be a mistake to say that this is what the mantra means. Such a phrase cannot give the real, much less still the total, meaning of the mantra. At best it gives just a facet – and not even the most important facet – of the meaning.

It is even more difficult to give an exact meaning to a word such as *svāhā*, which often comes at the end of mantras. Its conventional meaning is something like 'so be it', or 'that's it'. However, again it would be wrong to say that this is its meaning in the mantra. Perhaps the most we can say is that it carries connotations of affirmation, well-being, and success. And even then it does not carry these connotations for everyone. '*Svāhā*' occurs a great deal in Brahminical rituals and for this reason it would spark off the wrong sort of feelings amongst most Indian Buddhists, especially ex-Untouchables. It would be rather like Western Buddhists saying 'amen' in a puja. There is nothing wrong with saying 'amen' if you take it literally – it just means 'yes' – but the connotations and associations are all wrong.

Many mantras contain no words with defined meanings at all. The Tārā mantra, for instance, consists of a series of modulations of the vocative form of the name Tārā, i.e. 'Tāre'. There is no analysable meaning; reciting the mantra is apparently just juggling with the sound of the name. But mantras are not simply names either – certainly not in the sense of mere labels. Some mantras do include the personal name of the Buddha or Bodhisattva to which they 'belong', or variations on that name, but others do not.

Thirdly, and most importantly, a mantra is a sound symbol of a particular divinity, such as a Buddha or Bodhisattva. If that divinity could become a sound, which according to Tantric Buddhism it can and does, then that sound is the mantra. Just as the visualized image is the equivalent of the divinity in terms of form and colour, so the mantra is the equivalent in terms of sound. The mantra can therefore be thought of as the true, inherent name of the divinity – regardless of whether it includes the divinity's conventional name. When we call a person by name, he comes; similarly, when we invoke a particular divinity with a mantra, that divinity manifests, becomes present.

Fourthly, using the term 'mantra' in the strict Tantric meaning, a mantra is given by the guru to the disciple at the time of bestowing a Tantric initiation. Usually the disciple repeats the mantra three times after the guru and through this ritual, spiritual energy is 'transmitted'. If a mantra is not given in this way, it is not truly a mantra. People may read mantras in books, learn them, and start to recite them, and they may even get some benefit from doing so, but what they are reciting is not a mantra. Part of the meaning of mantra is that the practitioner is empowered to use it by the guru, that is, by a more spiritually advanced person than the practitioner with whom he or she is in communication. If it is picked up in any other way, it may be good religious practice, but it is not Tantric recitation of a mantra. Incidentally, the guru may not necessarily be a human living guru. It is possible to receive mantras in dreams or in the course of meditation from a guru-figure.

Fifthly and lastly, a mantra is something that is repeated. It should be repeated regularly and earnestly over a long period, until eventually inner repetition becomes spontaneous, no longer requiring conscious effort. But if it is neglected, the energy originally transmitted by the guru will gradually be lost.

The recitation of mantras occupies an extremely important place in Tantric Buddhism. The Tantra was in fact originally known as the Mantrayāna, 'the way of the mantras'. This distinguished it from the Mahāyāna which was then known as the Pāramitāyāna, 'the way of the practice of the Perfections'. The term Vajrayāna came into use much later, to refer to the more advanced and radical development of the Tantric tradition. It is said that progress is more rapid in the Mantrayāna than in the Pāramitāyāna. The practice of the Perfections – giving, morality, patience, vigour, meditation, and wisdom – represents a complete scheme of ethical and spiritual development, but it appeals more to the conscious mind, at least in the early stages. It is an arduous but intelligible path of practice. The Mantrayāna, on the other hand, is directed much more to the unconscious mind. It aims directly to contact the spiritual forces which are latent in the depths of the mind – forces which are ultimately different aspects of the Enlightened mind. These aspects of the Enlightened mind are personified, or, more accurately, crystallized, in the forms of Buddhas, Bodhisattvas and other deities. And according to the Tantra they can be contacted through the practice of visualization of form and colour together with invocation and mantric sound.

The chanting of mantras comes at the end of the Sevenfold Puja. At this point we have already experienced ourselves in relation to the Enlightened mind in a number of ways, represented by the progressive sequence of the seven stages of the puja, and we have felt the strong spiritual emotions and ardent aspirations aroused by seeing ourselves in relation to Enlightenment. Even so, the Enlightened mind may still seem to us to be something quite remote, something of a different order. The chanting of mantras represents the actual presence of Enlightenment, of the Buddhas and Bodhisattvas, in the world and in our own being. It indicates the real possibility for our energies to be radically transformed so that we can make manifest the qualities of Enlightenment which are buried deep within us, and become a channel for the arising of the bodhicitta. This Tantric touch can lift the whole puja to an altogether higher level.

Although the sevenfold form of puja comes from the Mahāyāna tradition, the version used within the FWBO deliberately includes elements of the Hīnayāna and the Vajrayāna as well. This is not just for the sake of having all three traditional yānas represented but because of the spiritual efficacy of doing so.

So now let us meet the eight Buddhas and Bodhisattvas whose mantras are chanted at the end of the Sevenfold Puja. The first three are what the Tibetans call the three 'Family Protectors', the Bodhisattvas representing Compassion (Avalokiteśvara), Wisdom (Mañjuśrī), and Spiritual Energy (Vajrapāṇi).[20]

The Avalokiteśvara mantra is the most widely known and chanted of all mantras. Avalokiteśvara is the quintessence of compassion, the chief Bodhisattva in the Lotus family of which the Buddha Amitābha is the head. He is the active expression of the boundless love which Amitābha represents. He is sometimes envisaged as red, like Amitābha, especially in the form known as Padmapāṇi ('lotus in hand'), but he is more often depicted as pure shining white, most commonly in his four-armed and thousand-armed forms. The many arms of this extraordinary figure reach out in all directions to help suffering beings. His name means 'the lord who looks down', who sees the suffering of beings so that he may respond.

Just as Avalokiteśvara is the embodiment of absolute compassion, so Mañjuśrī, also known as Mañjughoṣa, is the embodiment of transcendental wisdom. Mañjuśrī appears in the form of a beautiful sixteen-year-old youth, a deep, rich yellow in colour and clad in the usual silks and jewels of a Bodhisattva. His right arm is uplifted and he flourishes above his head the flaming sword of wisdom with which he cuts the bonds of karma and ignorance. In his left hand, which he presses to his heart, he holds a book of the Perfection of Wisdom. In keeping with his manifestation of supreme wisdom he is known also as 'the lord of speech' and seen as the patron of the arts and sciences.

In order to convey something of the boundless energy which Vajrapāṇi embodies, he is most often depicted in wrathful form, although he also has peaceful forms. In the more popular wrathful form he is dark blue like the midnight sky, stout and strong with thick, short limbs and a protuberant belly. His powerful body is generally naked except for ornaments of human bone, and he wears a crown of human skulls. He has three eyes – the third being in the middle of his forehead – which glare ferociously. Surrounded by a halo of flames, he is trampling triumphantly on two figures which represent ignorance and craving, the evils which he has destroyed. His right arm is raised and in his right hand he grasps, as though ready to hurl it, the vajra or diamond-thunderbolt. Indeed his name means 'thunderbolt in hand'.

Following on from the three Family Protectors, there is Tārā, the principal feminine Bodhisattva or Buddha form. The mantra which we chant is particularly that of Tārā in her form of Green Tārā. The other most popular form, that of White Tārā, has a somewhat extended version of the same mantra. Like Avalokiteśvara, Tārā manifests especially the quality of compassion, and her hands make gestures symbolizing giving and the dispelling of fear. Her name means 'the one who ferries across', that is to say the one who ferries beings across the river of birth and death, the river of saṁsāra, to reach the further shore, which is nirvāṇa. The name Tārā is sometimes translated as 'saviouress', but this is perhaps misleading. Tārā represents more the attitude of helping people to help themselves.

Amitābha, whose mantra comes next, is the red Buddha of the western quarter. His name literally means 'infinite light' and he embodies not just light but warmth, the maturing power of great love, as symbolized by his deep, brilliant red colour. Amitābha's emblem, the lotus flower, symbolizes spiritual unfoldment and growth, a process which is nourished and fostered by love. His hands are in the mudra of meditation. Just as the sun sets in the west in a glorious blaze of red, so the mind withdraws from the cares of the everyday world, quiet but more alive than ever, as it enters a state of meditation.

The next mantra is that of Śākyamuni, the historical Buddha, the extraordinary human being who discovered and opened up for others the way to Enlightenment in our world-age. The central figure in the vast body of Buddhist teaching, devotional practice and art, Śākyamuni embodies all the innumerable and excellent Buddha-qualities. At the same time his presence reminds us that, as we say in the 'short puja':

The Buddha was born, as we are born.
What the Buddha overcame, we too can overcome;
What the Buddha attained, we too can attain.

Following on from Śākyamuni, we come to Padmasambhava, the archetypal guru. A part-historical, part-mythical figure, Padmasambhava was the single most important influence in the establishment of Buddhism in Tibet, where he is said to have subdued the local gods and demons and converted them to be protectors of the Dharma. He therefore represents among other things the ability to deal with and integrate powerful psychic forces. He is a heroic and vigorous figure. In his principal manifestation – he has many others – he is clad in very rich, colourful, and princely garments, and wears on his head the famous lotus cap which terminates in a vajra and a vulture's feather. He holds a skull cup and a golden vajra. In the crook of his left arm there is a long staff with streamers, surmounted by three severed human heads and a trident. His expression is benign and compassionate, although his smile is not without a touch of ferocity.

Finally there is the mantra of the Perfection of Wisdom, Prajñāpāramitā, which is in a way impersonal and may appeal to those who do not get on very well with 'personal' embodiments of the ideal. Although there *is* a figure of Prajñāpāramitā, she has a different mantra. The normal association of this mantra, which comes from the *Heart Sūtra*, is Prajñāpāramitā, or the Perfection of Wisdom, in the abstract rather than

Prajñāpāramitā as a deity that can be visualized. However, there is no hard and fast distinction.

The puja ends, then, with the Perfection of Wisdom, the sublime wisdom that goes beyond, 'holding to nothing whatever' as the *Heart Sūtra* says – the wisdom which is the essence of the Enlightenment of all the Buddhas. Dwelling in the radiance of this last mantra, in the accumulated radiance of all the mantras, we chant just four more words, each in more gentle and attenuated tones than the one before: '*oṁ, śānti, śānti, śānti....*' (oṁ, peace, peace, peace....). We experience perhaps a glimmering of that peace which is at once perfectly tranquil and utterly dynamic, brimming with energy and potential. We remain in silence for a short while, or, if we can, for a good long while, to absorb and rejoice in the excellent and propitious emotions aroused by the Sevenfold Puja.

•

NOTES AND REFERENCES

1 *Samādhi*: usually translated 'meditation', this word can stand for concentration, or (on a deeper level) the state of being fixed or established in Ultimate Reality. For more information, see Sangharakshita, *Vision and Transformation*, Windhorse, Glasgow 1990.

2 *The FWBO Puja Book: A Book of Buddhist Devotional Texts* (Windhorse, Glasgow 1990) contains the text of the Sevenfold Puja, the Short Puja, and other devotional verses, chants, and recitations used by the Friends of the Western Buddhist Order.

3 The Five Precepts are 'rules of training' the recitation of which, together with the Three Refuges (see chapter 8), is the formal act signifying that one is a Buddhist. Practising Buddhists try to observe the precepts in their lives. For a list of the Five Precepts see p.77.

4 For information about the life of Dhardo Rimpoche see Suvajra, *The Wheel and the Diamond*, Windhorse, Glasgow 1991.

5 *bhikkhu* (Pali): a Buddhist monk, traditionally a mendicant who begs for his food and teaches the Dharma.

6 *Rūpa* (Pali and Sanskrit): literally 'form'; a sculpted image of a Buddha or Bodhisattva.

7 Bodhicitta (Pali and Sanskrit): literally 'thought of Enlightenment'; more usefully translated as 'Will to Enlightenment'. See chapter 12, also

Sangharakshita, *The Meaning of Conversion in Buddhism*, Windhorse, Birmingham 1994.

8 See Śāntideva, *Bodhicaryāvatāra*, trans. Marion L. Matics, under the title *Entering the Path of Enlightenment*, Allen & Unwin, London 1970. See also Stephen Batchelor's translation from the Tibetan: *A Guide to the Bodhisattva's Way of Life*, Library of Tibetan Works and Archives, Dharamsala 1981.

9 Sangharakshita, *A Survey of Buddhism: Its Doctrines and Methods through the Ages*, 7th edition, Windhorse, Glasgow 1993, pp.442–444.

10 *Sūtra of Golden Light*, trans. R.E. Emmerick, Pali Text Society, London 1979. See also Sangharakshita's commentary on this sūtra, *Transforming Self and World*, Windhorse, Birmingham 1995.

11 Dīpankara is traditionally the Buddha who preceded the Buddha of our own era, Siddhartha Gautama, known in the lineage of Buddhas as Śākyamuni. The Bodhisattva Maitreya is the 'Buddha to come', the next in the lineage, who, according to tradition, will appear when the world has need of another Teacher.

12 Lama Anagarika Govinda studied Tibetan Buddhism and wrote several deeply perceptive books about it. See in particular *Foundations of Tibetan Mysticism*, Rider, London 1983, and his memoirs, *The Way of the White Clouds*, Rider, London 1984.

13 *Pāramitās*: the six perfections practised by a Bodhisattva, usually listed as generosity, ethics, patience or forbearance, energy or effort, meditation, and wisdom.

14 *Śrāmaṇera* precepts: the ten precepts undertaken by novice monks or *śrāmaṇeras* include the Five Precepts listed in chapter 8, with the modification that instead of undertaking to abstain from sexual misconduct, *śrāmaṇeras* undertake to refrain from all sexual activity. The remaining five precepts include abstaining from: eating after midday, music and dancing, luxurious beds, wearing garlands, scent, or jewellery, and handling money.

15 For more about the Ten Precepts observed by members of the Western Buddhist Order, see Sangharakshita, *The Ten Pillars of Buddhism*, Windhorse, Glasgow 1988.

16 For a fuller treatment of karma, including what it is not, see Sangharakshita, *Who Is the Buddha?*, Windhorse, Birmingham 1994.

17 *Saṁsāra*: the endless round of birth, death, and rebirth.

18 The *Mahā-parinibbāna Sutta* is contained in the *Dīgha-Nikāya*, Pali Text Society, London 1977.

19 For a commentary on this brief but vital sūtra, see Sangharakshita, *Wisdom Beyond Words*, Windhorse, Glasgow 1993.

20 For a fuller description of Buddha and Bodhisattva figures, with illustrations, see Vessantara, *Meeting the Buddhas*, Windhorse, Glasgow 1993.

•

INDEX

W

White Lotus Sūtra
  see Saddharma-puṇḍarīka Sūtra
worship   38, 51ff., 67, *see also* puja

Z

Zen   28

The Windhorse symbolizes the energy of the enlightened mind carrying the Three Jewels
– the Buddha, the Dharma, and the Sangha – to all sentient beings.
Buddhism is one of the fastest growing spiritual traditions in the Western world.
Throughout its 2,500-year history, it has always succeeded in adapting its mode of
expression to suit whatever culture it has encountered.
Windhorse Publications aims to continue this tradition as Buddhism comes to the West.
Today's Westerners are heirs to the entire Buddhist tradition, free to draw instruction and
inspiration from all the many schools and branches. Windhorse publishes works by
authors who not only understand the Buddhist tradition but are also familiar with
Western culture and the Western mind.

For orders and catalogues contact

WINDHORSE PUBLICATIONS

UNIT 1-316 THE CUSTARD FACTORY

GIBB STREET

BIRMINGHAM

B9 4AA

UK

WINDHORSE PUBLICATIONS (USA)

14 HEARTWOOD CIRCLE

NEWMARKET

NEW HAMPSHIRE

NH 03857

USA

Windhorse Publications is an arm of the Friends of the Western Buddhist Order, which has more than sixty centres on four continents. Through these centres, members of the Western Buddhist Order offer regular programmes of events for the general public and for more experienced students. These include meditation classes, public talks, study on Buddhist themes and texts, and 'bodywork' classes such as t'ai chi, yoga, and massage. The FWBO also runs several retreat centres and the Karuna Trust, a fundraising charity that supports social welfare projects in the slums and villages of India.

Many FWBO centres have residential spiritual communities and ethical businesses associated with them. Arts activities are encouraged too, as is the development of strong bonds of friendship between people who share the same ideals. In this way the FWBO is developing a unique approach to Buddhism, not simply as a set of techniques, less still as an exotic cultural interest, but as a creatively directed way of life for people living in the modern world.

If you would like more information about the FWBO please write to

LONDON BUDDHIST CENTRE	ARYALOKA
51 ROMAN ROAD	HEARTWOOD CIRCLE
LONDON	NEWMARKET
E2 OHU	NEW HAMPSHIRE
UK	NH 03857
	USA

ALSO FROM WINDHORSE

VESSANTARA
MEETING THE BUDDHAS:
A GUIDE TO BUDDHAS, BODHISATTVAS, AND TANTRIC DEITIES

Who are those benign or fierce beings of the Buddhist Indo-Tibetan tradition? Are they products of an Eastern imagination with no relevance to the West? Or are they real? And what have they got to do with us? This vivid and informed account guides us to the heart of this magical realm and introduces us to the miraculous beings who dwell there.
368 pages, 234 x 156, text illustrations and colour plates
ISBN 0 904766 53 5
paperback £13.99/$24

SANGHARAKSHITA
WHO IS THE BUDDHA?

Through the centuries the Buddha has fascinated many people, but what kind of a man was he? This book is a popular introduction to the Buddha as a historical figure and as an archetype.
176 pages, black and white line drawings, index
ISBN 0 904766 24 1
£6.99/$11.95

Orders and catalogues from
Windhorse Publications
Unit 1-316 The Custard Factory
Gibb Street
Birmingham
B9 4AA